WEEKEND MAKES

CROCHETED BAGS

25 QUICK AND EASY PROJECTS TO MAKE

WEEKEND MAKES

CROCHETED BAGS

25 QUICK AND EASY PROJECTS TO MAKE

EMMA OSMOND

THE GUILD OF MASTER CRAFTSMAN PUBLICATIONS

First published 2021 by
Guild of Master Craftsman Publications Ltd
Castle Place, 166 High Street, Lewes,
East Sussex, BN7 1XU

Text © Quail Publishing, 2021
Copyright in the Work © GMC Publications Ltd, 2021

ISBN 978-1-78494-618-0

Project Manager: Kerry Kimber
Managing Art Editor: Darren Brant
Art Editor: Jennifer Stephens
Editors: Honor Head, Jean Coppendale
Photographer: Quail Studio
Stylists: Steph Booth, Sarah Mosedale - Mose &

Colour origination by GMC Reprographics
Printed and bound in China

CONTENTS

INTRODUCTION

Welcome to *Weekend Makes – Crocheted Bags*. This is a collection of 25 exciting projects from different designers, each with their own style and flair, so you can create something special for yourself or as a gift.

Whether you're looking for a new skill or you've tried crochet already and are looking for ideas to take you to another level, there's plenty here to tempt you. Some bags are super quick and can be completed in just a few hours or so, while others will take a little longer, depending on your ability.

Each project is graded as 'Easy', 'Intermediate' or 'Requires Experience'. Basic craft skills are all you need for the really simple 'Easy' projects, which are suitable for beginners. The 'Intermediate' and 'Requires Experience' projects need a little more making-up and finishing skills, and may take a longer to make. Whatever your level, the techniques section at the front of the book will give you all the information about the skills you will need to complete each project.

The 25 crocheted bags in this book are chic and practical. I have had so much fun curating these projects and I really hope you enjoy making them.

Emma Osmond

TOOLS AND MATERIALS

HOOKS

Crochet hooks come in a range of different sizes, shapes and materials. All the patterns specify the size of hook to use, although you may find you will need to use a larger or smaller hook to get the correct tension.

YARN

Yarn can be made from many different types of natural and artificial fibres and comes in a variety of weights and finishes. The patterns specify what type of yarn to use and how much you will need to complete each project.

SCISSORS

Choose sharp embroidery scissors to trim off all the yarn ends.

STITCH MARKERS

Split rings or loops can be placed onto your crochet to mark your place on a pattern or to indicate the beginning of a round.

TAPESTRY / DARNING NEEDLE

Sewing needles with blunt ends and large eyes are recommended for sewing up seams.

DRESSMAKERS' PINS

Glass-headed steel pins are ideal for blocking out crochet as they will not rust if they get wet. Long pins with decorative heads are useful for pinning crochet seams together as the heads can be easily seen.

TAPE MEASURE

Some crochet patterns will ask you to work a number of rows or rounds, while others tell you to work to a specific length. A tape measure is also required to check your tension squares.

ROW COUNTER

A row counter will help you to keep track of how many rows or rounds you have worked.

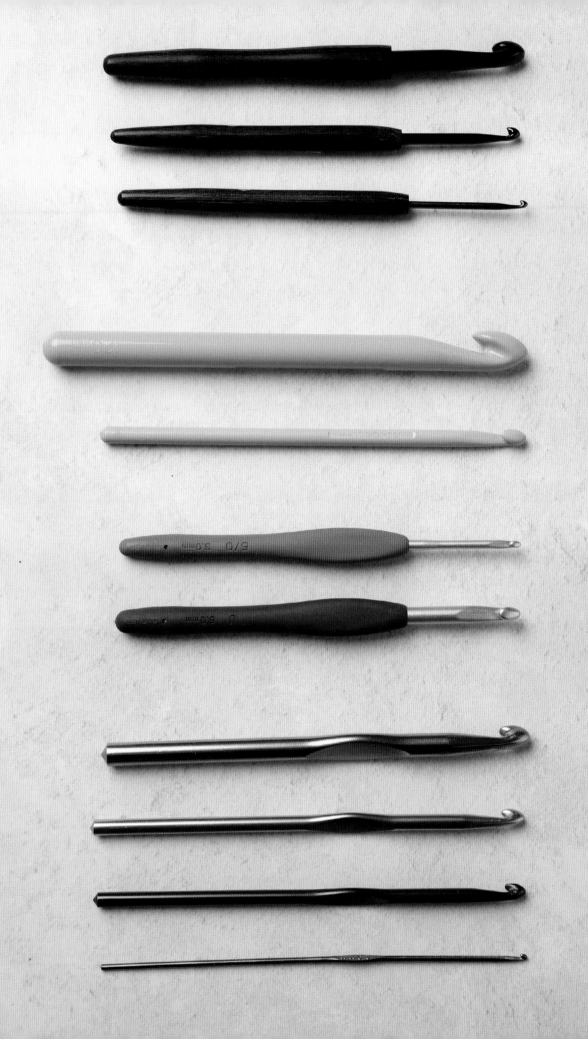

CROCHET TERMINOLOGY AND ABBREVIATIONS

CROCHET HOOK SIZES AND CONVERSIONS

The patterns in this book are written using UK crochet terms. Many US terms differ, so to avoid confusion, the tables below and right show conversions for hook sizes, terminology and abbreviations.

US SIZES	METRIC SIZES (mm)
-	2.0
B/1	2.25
-	2.5
C/2	2.75
-	3.0
D/3	3.25
E/4	3.5
F/5	3.75
G/6	4.0
7	4.5
H/8	5.0
I/9	5.5
J/10	6.0
K/10½	6.5
-	7.0
L/11	8.0
M/13	9.0
N/15	10.0

UK		US	
slip stitch	ss	slip stitch	ss
double crochet	dc	single crochet	sc
half treble crochet	htr	half double crochet	hdc
treble crochet	tr	double crochet	dc
double treble crochet	dtr	treble crochet	tr

ABBREVIATIONS

Shortened forms of terms are included to make the patterns more concise. This is a list of the most common UK crochet terms and their abbreviations.

beg	beginning		inc	increase
CC	contrast colour		m	metre(s)
ch	chain		MB	make bobble
ch-sp	chain space		MC	main colour
cm	centimetre(s)		mm	millimetre(s)
corner-sp	corner space		patt	pattern
dc	double crochet		rem	remain(ing)
dc2tog	double crochet two stitches together (decrease by one stitch)		RS	right side
			sp	space
			ss	slip stitch
dec	decrease		st(s)	stitch(es)
dk	double knit (yarn weight)		tr	treble
dtr	double treble		tr2tog	treble crochet two stitches together (decrease by one stitch)
foll	following			
g	gram(s)		trtr	treble treble
hdc	half double crochet		WS	wrong side
htr	half treble crochet		yd	yard(s)
in	inch(es)			

CROCHET BASICS

TENSION

The tension (also known as the 'gauge') varies in crochet, depending on how loose or tight you work. It is important to work in the tension specified in the pattern to ensure success. To do this, crochet a tension square by following the stitch pattern provided in the instructions. Make five to ten more stitches and rows than required. Mark out the central 4in (10cm) square with pins. If you have too many stitches or rows in 4in (10cm), make another tension square using a thicker hook. If you have too few stitches or rows in 4in (10cm), try again using a finer hook.

BLOCKING (PRESSING)

Block out each piece of crochet and follow the instructions on the ball band to press the project pieces, omitting the ribs. If the ball band indicates that the fabric is not to be pressed, then covering the blocked-out fabric with a damp white cotton cloth and leaving it to stand will have the desired effect. Darn in all ends neatly along the selvedge edge or a colour join, as appropriate.

MAKING UP (SEWING)

Pin the pieces together, carefully matching the colour and texture variations where necessary. Use a back stitch or mattress stitch for all the main crochet seams (see page 25), unless otherwise stated.

CROCHET STITCHES

MAKING A SLIP KNOT

Crochet begins by making a slip knot on the hook.

1 Make a loop in the end of the yarn and use the hook to pull a second loop through. Pull the end gently to secure the knot on the hook.

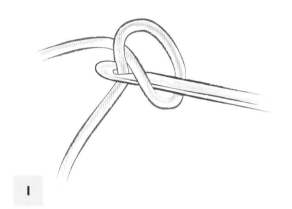

CHAIN STITCH

Most crochet projects begin with making a length of chain stitch, often referred to as the foundation row. The pattern will tell you how many chains to make.

1 Starting with a slip knot on your hook, wrap the yarn from back to front over the hook and pull the yarn through to form a new stitch.

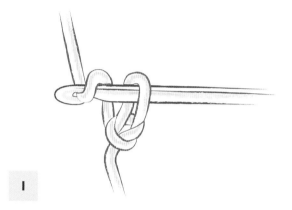

2 Repeat to make as many chains as specified in the pattern.

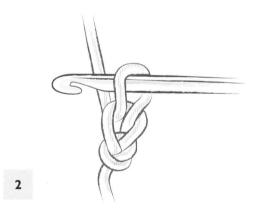

Tip:
When counting chains, the slip knot and the loop on the hook do not count.

SLIP STITCH

This is the smallest crochet stitch, and it is used to join, shape and carry yarn.

1 Insert the hook under two strands of the chain specified in the pattern. Wrap the yarn over the hook from back to front and pull the yarn through all the stitches on the hook.

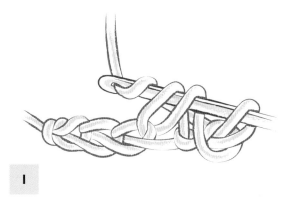

Tip:
Unless otherwise specified, always insert the hook through the top two strands of the chain you are working into.

DOUBLE CROCHET

This is a short, thick stitch, which creates a dense and flexible fabric.

1 Insert the hook from front to back through the second chain from the hook. Wrap the yarn over the hook from back to front and pull the yarn through the chain only. You now have two loops on the hook.

2 Bring the yarn over the hook again and pull it through both loops on the hook.

3 This leaves one loop on the hook and completes the stitch.

HALF TREBLE CROCHET

The half treble crochet is halfway between double crochet and treble crochet. It produces a firm, durable fabric that is used in many patterns.

1 Wrap the yarn over the hook from back to front.

2 Insert the hook into the chain specified by the pattern. Wrap the yarn around the hook again and pull it through the chain only. You will then have three loops on the hook.

3 Wrap the yarn around the hook again and pull it through all the loops on the hook.

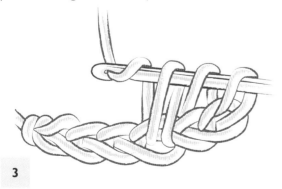

4 This leaves one loop on the hook and completes the stitch.

TREBLE CROCHET

Treble crochet produces tall stitches, which can create a more open fabric in no time at all.

I Wrap the yarn over the hook from back to front.

2 Insert the hook into the chain specified by the pattern. Wrap the yarn around the hook again and pull it through the chain only. You will then have three loops on the hook.

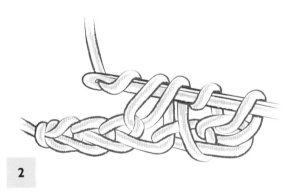

3 Wrap the yarn around the hook again and pull it through two loops only. You now have two loops on the hook.

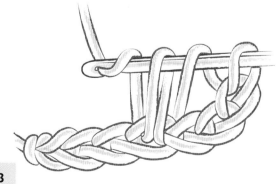

4 Wrap the yarn around the hook and pull it through the remaining loops.

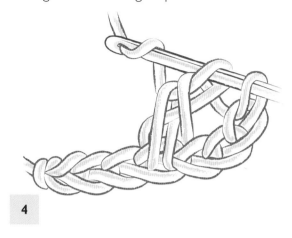

5 This leaves one loop on the hook and completes the stitch.

DOUBLE TREBLE CROCHET

Double treble crochet creates a loose, holey fabric and is commonly used in lacy designs.

1 Wrap the yarn over the hook from back to front twice.

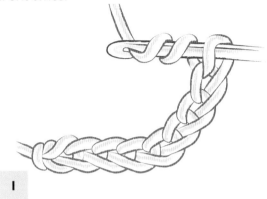

2 Insert the hook into the chain specified by the pattern. Wrap the yarn around the hook again and pull it through the chain only. You now have three loops on the hook.

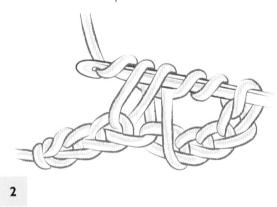

3 Wrap the yarn around the hook again and pull it through two loops only. You now have two loops on the hook.

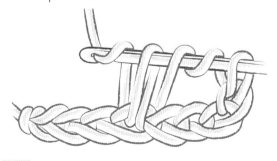

4 Wrap the yarn around the hook again and pull it through two loops only. You now have two loops on the hook.

5 Wrap the yarn around the hook and pull it through the remaining loops.

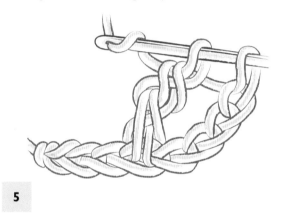

6 This leaves one loop on the hook and completes the stitch.

WORKING IN ROWS

Crochet can be worked flat by going backwards and forwards in rows. Extra chains are worked at each edge to bring the hook up to the same height as the first stitch of the next row. The list below shows the standard number of chain stitches needed to make a turn for each type of crochet stitch.

Double – 1 chain
Half treble – 2 chains
Treble – 3 chains
Double treble – 4 chains

MAKING A RING

Crochet can be worked in rounds from the centre, starting with a foundation ring of chain stitches (see also Magic Ring, page 22).

1 Make a row of chains as specified in the pattern.

2 Join the ring by making a slip stitch (see page 17) into the first chain.

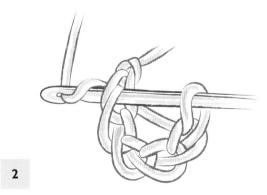

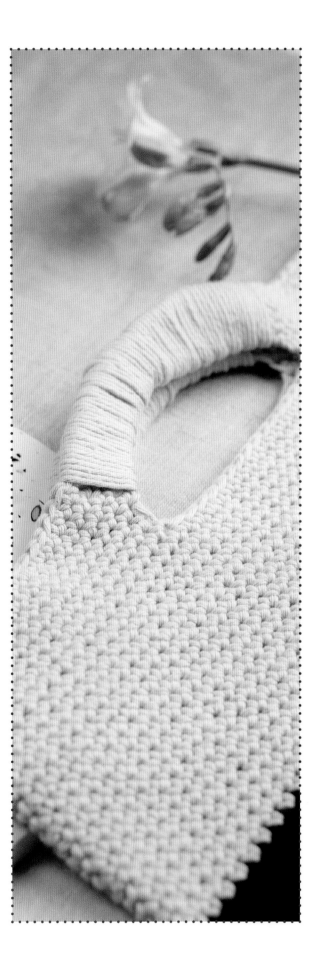

WORKING INTO A RING

Moving on from making a ring, you will need to start working stitches into the centre.

1 Make the appropriate starting chain, depending on the stitch you will be using (see page 21).

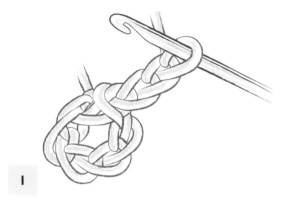

2 Insert the hook from the front to the back into the centre of the ring and work the stitch.

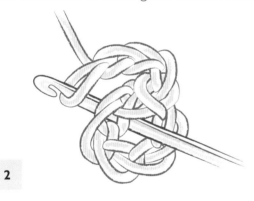

3 Continue working stitches into the centre of the ring. When you have worked around the full circle, finish off the round by working a slip stitch (see page 17) into the top of the starting chain worked at the beginning of the round.

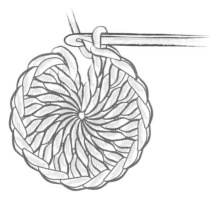

MAGIC RING

This is an alternative method for making a ring (see page 21) that allows you to close the centre hole.

1 Make a slip knot, but do not pull it tight around the hook.

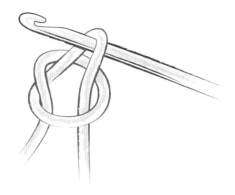

2 Wrap the yarn around the hook and pull it through the loop on your hook.

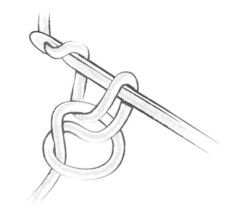

3 Work the first round of stitches into the ring.

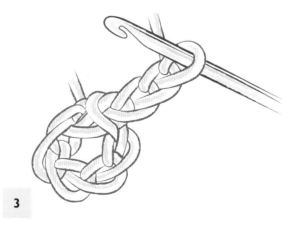

4 Pull the end tight to close the hole.

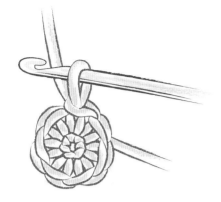

SHAPING – INCREASING

Increasing in between stitches is achieved by working two or more stitches into one stitch.

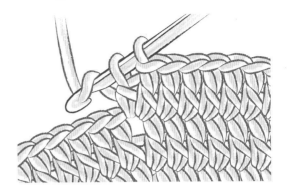

SHAPING – DECREASING

Stitches can be decreased by working two or more incomplete stitches together as if they were one.

1 Work the stitch until there are two loops on the hook. Then, work a second stitch, again leaving this incomplete so you now have three loops on the hook.

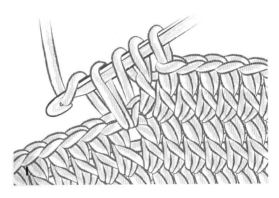

2 Wrap the yarn around the hook and pull it through all the remaining loops to finish the decrease.

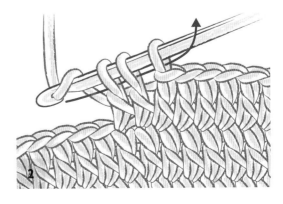

JOINING IN A NEW YARN

1 Leave the last stitch incomplete so you have two loops on your hook. Wrap the new yarn around the hook.

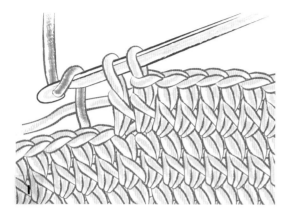

2 Pull the new yarn through the two loops to complete the stitch, and then continue working in the new colour.

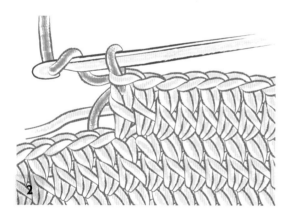

FASTENING OFF

1 To fasten off, cut the yarn about 4in (10cm) from the last stitch and pull the end through the last stitch. Pull the yarn to secure.

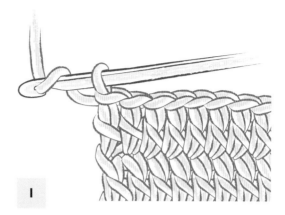

JOINING SEAMS

Sewn back-stitch seam

With right sides facing, hold the seam together, pinning if necessary. Sew along the edge with the matching yarn.

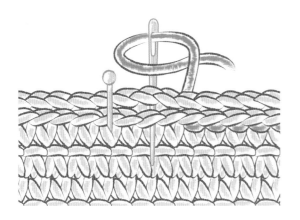

Mattress stitch / woven seam

With the right sides facing down, and the edges to be joined lying next to each other, use a tapestry needle threaded with matching yarn to weave in and out of the stitches.

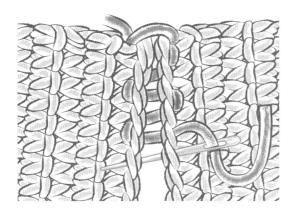

Slip stitch crochet seam

With right sides facing, work a row of slip stitches (see page 17) through both sides.

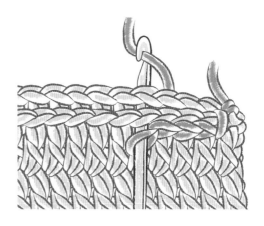

KNOT BAG
DESIGNED BY AMY PARKER

Sometimes you only need a small bag, but what about when you don't want a cross-body or clutch bag? This Knot Bag is the perfect solution. Small yet roomy enough to hold all your essentials, it has two handles that overlap to create a knot-like effect, which helps to keep your belongings safe.

SKILL LEVEL: INTERMEDIATE

YOU'LL NEED

YARN
No. 4 medium-weight yarn
(shown in Wool and the Gang Billie Jean)
A – 1 x 100g Dirty Denim
B – 1 x 100g Raw Denim

HOOK
4.5mm (US 7)

HABERDASHERY
2 x stitch markers
Large-eyed darning needle

KNOT BAG

SIZE
Approximately 8in (20cm) wide × 11in (28cm) long (measured from base to top of longest handle).

TENSION
15sts and 7.5 rows to 4in (10cm), measured over treble crochet, after blocking, using 4.5mm (US 7) hook.

METHOD
SPECIAL INSTRUCTIONS

Pull the yarn – pull the working yarn to create a large loop so that the open stitch will not unravel when you leave it to work the other colour. Tighten the loop around the hook when you pick up the colour to work the next row.

Adjustable loop – wrap the yarn around your index finger, over the top of the finger anticlockwise and all the way around the finger. Slide the loop off your finger and work the sts for the first round into this loop. Pull the tail to close.

3ch counts as a tr throughout.

SIDE 1

Row 1: Using yarn A, make an adjustable loop, 3ch, 5tr into the loop, pull the yarn, do not close the loop.

Row 2: Using yarn B, ss to loop, 3ch, 5tr into loop, pull the yarn to close the loop.

Row 3: Pick up yarn A, 2tr into top of 3ch of yarn B, place a stitch marker in the top of the first tr, 2tr into each of the yarn B tr, pull the yarn. 12tr counting from the stitch marker.

Row 4: With yarn B, repeat Row 3.

Row 5: Pick up yarn A, remove the stitch marker, 2tr into the first tr, place the stitch marker into the top of the first tr, 1tr, *2tr into tr, 1tr into the next tr; repeat from * to end, pull the yarn. 18tr.

Row 6: With yarn B, repeat Row 5.

Row 7: Pick up yarn A, remove the stitch marker, 2tr into the first tr, place the stitch marker in the top of the first tr, 2tr, *2tr into the next tr, 2tr; repeat from * to the end, pull the yarn. 24tr.

Row 8: With yarn B, repeat Row 7.

Row 9: Pick up yarn A, remove the stitch marker, 2tr into the first tr, place the stitch marker in the top of the first tr, 3tr, *2tr into the next tr, 3tr; repeat from * to the end, pull the yarn. 30tr.

Row 10: With yarn B, repeat Row 9.

Row 11: Pick up yarn A, remove the stitch marker, 2tr into the first tr, place the stitch marker in the top of the first tr, 4tr, *2tr into the next tr, 4tr; repeat from * to the end, pull the yarn. 36tr.

Row 12: With yarn B, repeat Row 11.

Row 13: Pick up yarn A, remove the stitch marker, 2tr into the first tr, place the stitch marker in the top of the first tr, 5tr, *2tr into next tr, 5tr; repeat from * to the end, pull the yarn. 42tr.

Row 14: With yarn B, repeat Row 13.

Row 15: Pick up yarn A, remove the stitch marker, 2tr into the first tr, place the stitch marker in the top of the first tr, 6tr, *2tr into the next tr, 6tr; repeat from * to the end, pull the yarn. 48tr.

Row 16: With yarn B, repeat Row 15.

Row 17: Pick up yarn A, remove the stitch marker, 2tr into the first tr, place the stitch marker in the top of the first tr, 3tr, 2htr, 2dc, ss into the next tr.
Fasten off.

Row 18: Pick up yarn B, remove the stitch marker, 2tr into the first tr, 7tr, *2tr into the next tr, 7tr; repeat until there are 27tr, counting from the stitch marker, place the stitch marker, 2tr into the next tr, 3tr, 2htr, 2dc, ss into the next tr.
Fasten off.

SIDE 2
Repeat Rows 1–18, beginning with yarn B.

MAKING UP
Keeping the stitch markers in place, press the two sides of the bag as described in Crochet Basics (see page 14), ensuring the width (diameter) measures 8in (20cm). Place the RS together (WS facing out). Position the edges with the stitch markers at the 'top' of the work and lining up with the final ss on the opposite sides.

Turn the work so the WS of side 1 is facing you. Sew from ss of yarn A, moving clockwise and stopping at the stitch marker in yarn B. Turn the bag inside out so the RS is now facing out.

HANDLES
First handle
Start at the stitch maker in the yarn A section on side 2 (next to the side seam).

Row 1: Using yarn A, 3ch, 3tr, 3htr, 3dc. Turn.

Row 2: 2ch, 2dc, 3htr, 4tr. Turn.

Row 3: 3ch, 9tr. Turn.

Rows 4–17: Repeat Row 3.

Row 18: 2ch, 2dc, 3htr, 4tr. Turn.

Row 19: 3ch, 3tr, 3htr, 3dc.
Fasten off, leaving a long tail.

Thread the tail through a darning needle and sew the handle to the opposite side, starting at the stitch marker in yarn A and working towards the side seam.

Second handle
Start at the stitch marker in the yarn B section (next to the side seam). With yarn B, work as for the first handle.

Weave in the ends.

BEACH BAG
DESIGNED BY SAMANTA FORNINO

This is a great bag for the summer. Its generous size means it will hold all you need for the beach, and it would be ideal for a serious shopping trip! You can make it in one colour or have fun with different colours to match your summer wardrobe.

SKILL LEVEL: EASY

YOU'LL NEED

YARN

No. 3 light-weight yarn
(shown in Ophelia Italy Cotton Gemma)
A – 3 x 50g Turquoise 015
B – 3 x 50g Sky Blue Baby 016
C – 1 x 50g Cream 002

HOOK

3.5mm (US E/4)

HABERDASHERY

Large-eyed darning needle

BEACH BAG

SIZE

Approximately 15¾in (40cm) square (excluding handles).

TENSION

20sts and 10 rows to 4in (10cm), measured over treble crochet using a 3.5mm (US E/4) hook.

METHOD

SPECIAL INSTRUCTIONS

Knit stitch – insert the hook into the post of the next stitch (in the 'V'), yarn over and pull through a loop, yarn over and pull through the two loops on the hook.

SIDE PANEL (MAKE 2)

Using a 3.5mm hook and yarn A, make 94ch.

Row 1 (RS): 1tr into the 3rd chain from the hook, 1tr into each ch to the end, turn. 92sts.

Rows 2–5: 3ch (count as a st), 1tr into each st to the end. Turn.

Rows 6–16: 3ch (count as a st), *1tr, miss 1tr, 1tr; rep from * to the last st, 1tr, turn. 47sts.

Change to yarn B.

Rows 17–33: 3ch (count as a st), *1tr, miss 1tr, 1tr; rep from * to the last st, 1tr, turn. 47sts.

Change to yarn C.

Rows 34–38: 3ch (count as a st), *1tr, miss 1tr, 1tr; rep from * to the last st, 1tr, turn. 47sts.

Row 39: 3ch (count as a st), *1tr, 1tr into the next ch-sp, 1tr; rep from * to last st, 1tr, turn. 92sts.

STRAPS (MAKE 2)

Begin knit st.

Row 40: 1ch (do not count as st), 25knit st, miss 42tr, 100ch, 25knit st. 50sts.

Row 41: 1ch (do not count as st), 25knit st, 100tr, 25 knit st. 150sts.

Fasten off.

MAKING UP

Sew the bottom and two sides together using a mattress stitch (see page 25), leaving the top open.

CHECKED RUCKSACK

DESIGNED BY EMMA WRIGHT

This is the statement rucksack! A great project if you want to broaden your skills and do some crochet colour work, especially if you are a beginner at using different coloured yarns in one project. The check pattern is simple yet eye-catching.

SKILL LEVEL: INTERMEDIATE

YOU'LL NEED

YARN

No. 4 medium-weight yarn
(shown in Paintbox Yarns Cotton Aran)
A – 2 x 50g Pure Black 602

No. 3 lightweight yarn
(shown in Debbie Bliss Cotton Denim DK)
B – 1 x 100g Charcoal 01
C – 1 x 100g Milk 06

HOOKS

4mm (US G/6)
5mm (US H/8)

HABERDASHERY

Large-eyed darning needle

CHECKED RUCKSACK

SIZE

10in (25cm) wide × 11½in (29cm) high
Handle: 7in (18cm)
Straps: 19½in (50cm)

TENSION

18tr sts and 8.5tr rows to 4in (10cm) using a
4mm hook.

METHOD

Pattern note – when a new colour is introduced,
lay the other colours over the hook, towards
the back of the work, and trap them inside
each tr worked to trail non-used yarns across
the row. Then, when needed, pick up the new
colour and lay the old colour behind, as you
did previously.

BAG
Using the 4mm hook and yarn A, make 46ch.

Row 1: 1tr into 3rd ch from hook, 1tr into next
3ch/sts, add yarn B (see pattern note, left),
*1tr into next 4sts in yarn B, 1tr into next
4sts in yarn A; rep from * to the end,
turn. 44sts.
Row 2: 2ch in yarn A (doesn't count as a st), 1tr
into the next 4sts in yarn A, *1tr into the next
4sts in yarn B, 1tr into the next 4 sts in yarn A;
rep from * to the end, turn.
Row 3: Add yarn C, 2ch in yarn C (doesn't count
as a st), 1tr into the next 4 sts in yarn C, *1tr
into the next 4sts in yarn A, 1tr into the next
4sts in yarn C; rep from * to the end, turn.
Row 4: As Row 3.
These four rows set checked tr patt.

Continue working in the checked tr patt until the
work measures approximately 21in (54cm). End
with Row 2 of the checked tr patt completed
(to mirror the beginning of the pattern).
Fasten off.

BAG FLAP

Using the 5mm hook and two strands of yarn C held together, make 11ch.

Row 1: 1tr into 3rd ch from the hook, 1 tr into the next 7ch, 5tr into the last ch (turning the corner to work on the opposite side of the beginning ch), miss 1ch, 1tr into the next 8ch, turn. 21sts.

Row 2: 2ch, 1tr into the next 8sts, 2tr into the next 5sts, 1tr into the next 8sts, turn. 26sts.

Row 3: 2ch, 1tr into the next 11sts, 2tr into the next 5sts, 1tr into the next 10sts, turn. 31sts.

Row 4: 2ch, 1tr into the next 13sts, 2tr into the next 5sts, 1tr into the next 13sts, turn. 36sts.

Row 5: 2ch, 1tr into the next 13sts, 2tr into the next 10sts, 1tr into the next 13sts, turn. 46sts.

Row 6: 2ch, 1tr into every st, turn.

Row 7: 2ch, 1tr into the next 20sts, 2tr into the next 7sts, 1tr into the next 19sts, turn. 50sts.

Row 8: 2ch, 1tr into the next 23sts, (2tr into the next st, 1tr into the next st) 3 times, 2tr into the next st, 1tr into the next 23sts, turn. 54sts.

Row 9: 1ch, 1dc into every st.
Fasten off.

SIDE (MAKE 2)

Using the 5mm hook and 2 strands of yarn A held together, make 14ch.

Row 1: 1tr into 3rd ch from the hook, 1tr into the next 11ch, turn. 12sts.

Row 2: 2ch (does not count as a st), 1tr into every st.

Row 3: Repeat Row 2 only until the work measures approximately 10in (25cm), ending with the RS facing out.
Fasten off.

BAG HANDLE

Using the 5mm hook and 2 strands of yarn A held together, make 6ch.

Row 1: 1tr into 3rd ch from the hook, 1tr into the next 3ch, turn. 4sts.

Row 2: 2ch (does not count as a st), 1tr into every st.

Row 3: Repeat Row 2 only until your work measures approximately 7in (18cm), ending with the RS facing out.
Fasten off.

BAG STRAP (MAKE 2)

Using the 5mm hook and 2 strands of yarn A held together, make 6ch.

Row 1: 1tr into 3rd ch from the hook, 1tr into the next 3ch, turn. 4sts.

Row 2: 2ch (does not count as a st), 1tr into every st.

Row 3: Repeat Row 2 only until your work measures approximately 19½in (50cm), or the desired length, ending with the RS facing out.
Fasten off.

(continued overleaf)

MAKING UP

Fasten off all the loose ends.

Use the 5mm hook and two strands of yarn A held together, then dc. Join the bottom (beg ch) of both bag sides to the central point (centre three squares) of the bag body. Then use dc to join both seams of the bag sides to the bag body.

With the RS of the bag flap to the RS of the bag body (back of bag only), use dc to join together (seam sits inside the bag under the bag flap).

Use a large-eyed darning needle and any leftover yarn to join the bag handle to the centre point of the seam on the outside of the work, where the bag flap joins the bag body, leaving a 1½in (4cm) gap.

Using the large-eyed darning needle, join each bag strap to the top of the bag and then to the right-hand and left-hand corners of the bag back. Fasten off any loose ends.

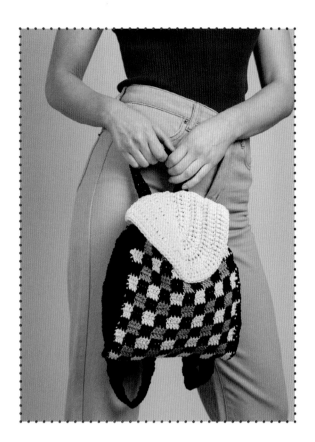

Tip
The straps are easily adjustable; you can just work them to your desired length. You may need a friend to help you to measure the perfect length. If you need longer straps, you may require another ball of yarn A.

JUTE CLUTCH

DESIGNED BY SAMANTA FORNINO

This clutch is worked in one piece. As well as a contrasting fold-over flap, it has the added detail of a wrist strap at the back. The combination of natural jute and cotton creates an interesting texture and makes it a stylish summer accessory for all occasions.

SKILL LEVEL: EASY

YOU'LL NEED

YARN

No. 2 lightweight jute yarn
(shown in Ophelia Italy Juta Natural)
A – 2 x 100g Natural 001

No. 3 lightweight cotton yarn
(shown in Ophelia Italy Stella)
B – 1 x 100g Coral 016

HOOK

5mm (US H/8)

HABERDASHERY

1 x 1in (25mm) metal snap button
2 x stitch markers
Large-eyed darning needle

JUTE CLUTCH

SIZE

Approximately 11in (28cm) wide × 6in (15cm) high.

TENSION

12sts and 16 rows to 4in (10cm), measured over double crochet using the 5mm hook and two strands of A held together.

METHOD

SPECIAL INSTRUCTIONS

Single crochet spike stitch – insert your hook into the base of the next stitch, yarn over and pull up a loop so that the hook is horizontal with the top of the stitch. Make sure the loop is the same height as the stitch and keep the stitches loose. Yarn over and pull through both loops.

CLUTCH

Using the 5mm hook and 2 strands of yarn A, make 35ch.

Row 1(RS): 1dc into 2nd chain from the hook, 1dc into each ch to the end, turn. 34sts.

Rows 2–50: 1ch (do not count as st), 1dc into every st to the end, turn. Place markers in each end of Row 41.

Change to yarn B.

Rows 51–66: 1ch (do not count as st), *1dc, 1 spike stitch (see Special Instructions, left); rep from * to the end, turn.

Fasten off.

WRIST STRAP

Using 5mm (US H/8) hook and yarn A, make 35ch.

Row 1 (RS): Working into one side of ch only, 1dc into 2nd chain from the hook, 1dc into each ch to the end, turn. 34sts.

Rows 2–4: 1ch (do not count as st), 1dc into st to the end, turn.

Change to yarn B.

Row 5: 1ch (do not count as st), 1dc into st to the end.
Fasten off.
Rejoin yarn B to the opposite side of ch and repeat Row 5.
Fasten off.

MAKING UP
Press as described in Crochet Basics (see page 14).

With the RS facing, fold Row 1 of the panel to the markers at Row 41. With the yarn B section (Rows 51–66) folded to form the closing at the front, face the back of the bag to you. Pin the strap to the back of the clutch so that the bottom of the strap is at the centre. Sew the sides of the strap to the sides of the back of the clutch.

Sew the side panels to the markers, leaving the top open.

Sew snap buttons to the centre front of the bag.

ROUND RAFFIA BAG

DESIGNED BY EMMA WRIGHT

Sure to liven up your spring or summer wardrobe, this bag is made with raffia and a strand of black linen. You could try swapping the black for your favourite coloured yarn or a colour to complement a special outfit.

SKILL LEVEL: REQUIRES EXPERIENCE

YOU'LL NEED

YARN
No. 3 lightweight raffia yarn
(shown in Wool and the Gang Ra Ra Raffia)
A – 1 x 100g Desert Palm

No. 3 lightweight yarn
(shown in Erika Knight Studio Linen)
B – 2 x 50g Kumo 411

HOOK
6mm (US J/10)

HABERDASHERY
Large-eyed darning needle
Stitch marker
Dressmakers' pins

ROUND RAFFIA BAG

SIZE
12in (30 cm) wide x 17in (43cm) high.

TENSION
12sts and 15 rows to 4in (10cm), measured over double crochet using the 6mm hook.

METHOD

BAG PANEL (MAKE 2)
Using the 6mm hook and holding one strand each of yarn A and yarn B together, make 3ch; ss into 1st ch to form a ring.

Round 1: 6dc into centre of ring, place marker to indicate beg/end of each round. 6sts.

Round 2: 2dc into each st. 12sts.

Round 3: (1dc into next st, 2dc into next st) 6 times. 18sts.

Round 4: (1dc into next 2sts, 2dc into next st) 6 times. 24sts.

Round 5: (1dc into next 3sts, 2dc in next st) 6 times. 30sts.

Round 6: (1dc into next 4sts, 2dc into next st) 6 times. 36sts.

Round 7: (1dc into next 5sts, 2dc into next st) 6 times. 42sts.

Round 8: (1dc into next 6sts, 2dc into next st) 6 times. 48sts.

Round 9: (1dc into next 7sts, 2dc in next st) 6 times. 54sts.

Round 10: (1dc into next 8sts, 2dc into next st) 6 times. 60sts.

Round 11: (1dc into next 9sts, 2dc in next st) 6 times. 66sts.

Round 12: (1dc into next 10sts, 2dc into next st) 6 times. 72sts.

Round 13: (1dc into next 11sts, 2dc into next st) 6 times. 78sts.

Round 14: (1dc into next 12sts, 2dc into next st) 6 times. 84sts.

Round 15: (1dc into next 13sts, 2dc into next st) 6 times. 90sts.

Round 16: (1dc into next 14sts, 2dc into next st) 6 times. 96sts.

Round 17: (1dc into next 15sts, 2dc into next st) 6 times. 102sts.

Round 18: (1dc into next 16sts, 2dc into the next st) 6 times. 108sts.

HANDLE BASE
Using the 6mm hook and one strand each of yarn A and B together; continue as follows:
Row 1: 1dc into next 14sts, turn.
Row 2 (WS): 1ch, dc2tog, 1dc into next 10sts, dc2tog, turn. 12sts.
Row 3: 1ch, 1dc in every st, turn.
Row 4: 1ch, 2dc into next st, 1dc into every st to the last st, 2dc into the last st, turn. 14sts.

First side of handle
Using the 6mm hook and one strand each of yarn A and B together; continue as follows:
Row 1: 1ch, 1dc into next 3sts, dc2tog, turn. 4sts.
Rows 2–8: 1ch, 1dc into next 3sts, turn. End with the RS facing.
Row 9: 1ch, dc2tog, 1dc into next st, 2dc into next st, turn.
Row 10: 1ch, 2dc into next st, 1dc into next st, dc2tog, turn.
Rows 11 and 12: Repeat Rows 9 and 10.
Row 13: 1ch, dc2tog, 1dc into next 2sts, turn. 3sts.
Row 14: 1ch, dc2tog, 1dc into next st, turn. 2sts.
Row 15: 1ch, dc2tog.
Fasten off.

Second side of handle
Using the 6mm hook and one strand each of yarn A and B together; re-join yarn to last 5dc of 14sts at handle base as follows:
Row 1: Dc2tog, 1dc into next 3sts, turn. 4sts.
Rows 2–8: 1ch, 1dc into next 3sts, turn. End with the RS facing out.
Row 9: 1ch, 2dc into next st, 1dc into next st, dc2tog, turn.

Row 10: 1ch, dc2tog, 1dc into next st, 2dc into next st, turn.
Rows 11 and 12: Repeat Rows 2 and 3.
Row 13: 1ch, 1dc into next 2sts, dc2tog, turn. 3sts.
Row 14: 1ch, 1dc into next st, dc2tog, turn. 2sts.
Row 15: 1ch, dc2tog.
Fasten off. Sew handle together.

SIDE PANEL
Using the 6mm hook, make 7ch.
Row 1: 1ch, 1dc into every ch to the end, turn.
Row 2: 1ch, 1dc into every st to the end, turn.
Repeat Row 2 only until the side measures approximately 23½in (60cm).
Fasten off.

MAKING UP
With one bag panel and the side panel WS together, pin the side panel into place around the first bag front.

Using the 6mm hook, and one strand each of yarn A and yarn B held together, dc st, join the side panel to the bag.
Join the second bag panel to the side panel in the same way.

Long strap
Using the 6mm hook and one strand each of yarn A and yarn B held together, make 106ch.
Row 1: 1dc into 2nd ch from the hook, 1dc into every ch to the end. 105sts.
Fasten off.

Join each side of the long strap to the bag approximately ½in (1cm) from the bottom of the bag handle on the main part of back bag panel.
Sew in any loose ends.

BOBBLE BOX TOTE
DESIGNED BY EMMA WRIGHT

This oversized tote is perfect for those quick supermarket trips. It's roomy but stylish, and crocheting each bobble is wonderfully therapeutic. This bag has leather handles for durability, but you can experiment with other materials to suit your own taste.

SKILL LEVEL: EASY

YOU'LL NEED

YARN
No. 3 lightweight yarn
(shown in Rowan Creative Linen)
5 × 100g Straw 622

HOOK
5mm (US H/8)

HABERDASHERY
2 × 23½in (60cm) long leather handles
Large-eyed darning needle, sharp and
    strong enough to go through the
    leather strap
Dressmakers' pins

BOBBLE BOX TOTE

SIZE
15½in (40cm) wide × 18½in (47cm) high × 3in (8cm) deep.

TENSION
11tr5tog and dc sts × 12tr5tog and dc rows to 4in (10cm) using the 5mm hook.

METHOD
SPECIAL INSTRUCTIONS
Make bobble, treble 5 together (TR5tog/MB) – yarn over, insert the hook into the next st, pull the yarn through (3 loops on the hook), yarn over and pull the yarn through 2 loops only (2 loops on the hook). Repeat until you have added 5tr on your hook (6 loops on the hook), yarn over and pull through all 6 loops (1 loop on hook), 1ch to secure the bobble.

BAG (MAKE 2)
Using the 5mm hook, make 56ch.
Row 1 (RS): 1dc into 2nd ch from the hook, 1dc into every ch to the end, turn. 55sts.

Row 2: 1ch, 1htr into 1st st, *(Tr5tog/MB [see Special Instructions, left], 1htr into next st) 6 times, 1htr into next 2sts; rep from * twice more, (Tr5tog/MB, 1 htr into next st) 6 times, turn.
Row 3: 1ch, 1dc into every st, turn.
Row 4: 1ch, 1htr into next 2sts, *(Tr5tog/MB, 1htr into next st) 5 times, 1htr into next 4sts; rep from * twice more, (Tr5tog/MB, 1 htr into next st) 5 times, 1htr into last st, turn.
Row 5: 1ch, 1dc into every st to end, turn.
Row 6: 1ch, 1htr into next 3sts, *(Tr5tog/MB, 1htr into next st) 4 times, 1htr in next 2sts, Tr5tog/MB, 1htr into next 3sts; rep from * twice more, (Tr5tog/MB, 1htr into next st) 4 times, 1htr into last 2sts, turn.
Row 7: 1ch, 1dc into every st to the end, turn.
Row 8: 1ch, 1htr into next 4sts, *(Tr5tog/MB, 1htr into next st) 3 times, 1htr into next 2sts, (Tr5tog/MB, 1htr into next st) twice, 1htr into next 2sts; rep from * twice more, (Tr5tog/MB, 1htr into next st) 3 times, 1htr into next 3sts, turn.

Row 9: 1ch, 1dc into every st to end, turn.

Row 10: 1ch, 1htr into next st, Tr5tog/MB, 1htr into next 3sts, *Tr5tog/MB, 1htr into next st, Tr5tog/MB, 1htr into next 3sts, (Tr5tog/MB, 1htr into next st) 3 times, 1htr into next 2sts; rep from * twice more, Tr5tog/MB, 1htr into the next st, Tr5tog/MB, 1htr in the next 3sts, Tr5tog/MB, 1htr in the last st, turn.

These 10 rows set the bobble stitch pattern from the chart.

Row 11: Continue to follow the chart until all 28 rows are complete.

Row 12: Repeat Rows 1–28 again.

Row 13 (RS): 1ch, 1dc into every st to the end, turn.

Row 14: 1ch, 1htr into front loop only of every st, turn.

Fasten off.

(continued overleaf)

CHART

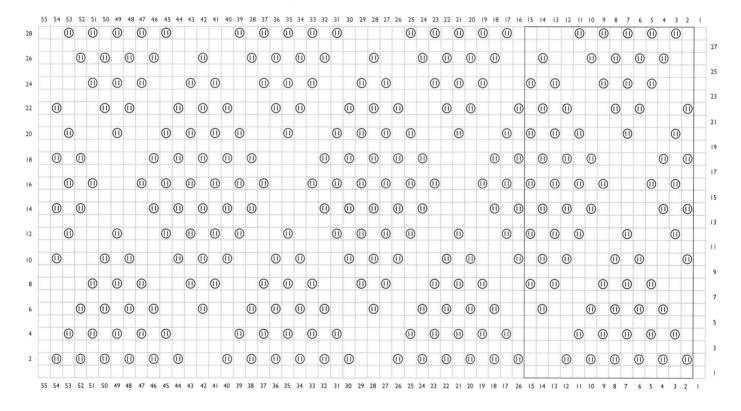

Key

☐ RS: knit
WS: purl

Ⓘ bobble

☐ bobble stitch repeat

SIDES

Using the 5mm hook, ch12.

Row 1: 1ch, 1dc into every ch to the end, turn.

Row 2: 1ch, 1dc into every st to the end, turn.

Rep Row 2 until the side measures approximately 53in (134cm) long or to fit right side, bottom and left side of one bag panel. Fasten off.

MAKING UP

With WS together, pin the side panel in place around the sides and bottom of the bag front.

Using the 5mm hook, dc these two pieces together. Join the bag back to the side panel in the same way.

Using a large-eyed sewing needle and any leftover yarn (or the studs provided with the handles), attach the leather handles approximately 4in (11cm) in from each edge. Fasten off any loose ends and block, as described in Crochet Basics (see page 14).

PATCHWORK BAG

DESIGNED BY AMY PARKER

Do you sometimes wish you had brought a bigger or smaller bag with you when you head out for the day? This clever pattern provides the best of both worlds, as the bag can be rolled down to become smaller, or unrolled so that you can fit more into it. It has a smart design and is smart to look at!

SKILL LEVEL: INTERMEDIATE

YOU'LL NEED

YARN

No. 3 lightweight cotton yarn
(shown in Rowan Summerlite DK)
A – 2 x 50g Seashell 466
B – 2 x 50g Summer 453
C – 2 x 50g Cantaloupe 456
D – 2 x 50g Lagoon 457

HOOK

3.5mm (US E/4)

HABERDASHERY

3yd x 1½in (3m x 38mm) cotton webbing
Sewing thread or scrap yarn the same
   colour as the cotton webbing
Large-eyed darning needle, sharp and
   strong enough to go through the
   cotton webbing
6 x pins or safety pins

PATCHWORK BAG

SIZE
Approximately 12in (30cm) long × 16in (41cm) wide.

TENSION
20sts and 9 rows to 4in (10cm), measured over treble crochet using a 3.5mm hook, after blocking (see Crochet Basics, page 14).

METHOD
SPECIAL INSTRUCTIONS
Make corner – into top of dtr work 2tr, dtr, 2tr. Tie knot – using a darning needle, sew the yarn through the middle of the final stitch to make a knot.

Adjustable loop – wrap the yarn around your index finger, over the top of the finger anticlockwise and all the way around the finger. Slide the loop off your finger and work the sts for the first round into this loop. Pull tightly closed and ss into 1st st. 3ch counts as a tr.

SQUARE (MAKE 96)
Row 1: Using yarn A, make an adjustable loop (see Special Instructions, left) 3ch, 2tr, dtr, (3tr, dtr) 3 times, ss into the top of the 3ch, fasten off, pull the tail to close the adjustable loop.
Row 2: Using yarn B, 3ch and tr into last dtr of Row 1, 3tr, make corner (see Special Instructions, left) 3tr, 2tr into the dtr, fasten off, tie knot.
Row 3: Using yarn C, 3ch into the top of the 3ch, 6tr, make corner, 7tr, fasten off, tie knot.
Row 4: Using yarn D, 3ch into the top of the 3ch, 8tr, make corner, 9tr, fasten off, tie knot.

MAKING UP
Block each square to measure 2 × 2in (5cm). See Crochet Basics on page 14.

PATCH (MAKE 24)
Place four squares with the WS facing out to form a larger square with the four yarn A sections in the centre and the yarn D rows forming a border around the edge. Using the 3.5mm crochet hook and yarn C, ss through the

backs of the stitches from the yarn D borders to the yarn A sections to join the top two squares. Continue on to the yarn A sections of the two lower squares, stitching to the yarn D borders of the lower two squares. Then, ss the horizontal seam in the same way to join the top two squares to the lower two squares.

With the 3.5mm crochet hook and yarn D, ss the squares together to form three strips of eight patches each. ss the three strips together. Fold the piece in half and ss the two sides, leaving the top open. With the RS facing out, and yarn D, ss along the open top edge of the bag for a finished edge.

STRAP
Taking care not to twist the strap, overlap the ends of the strap approximately 3in (7.5cm) and sew together. Place the strap around the bag with the strap seam on the bottom of the bag and the two sides of the strap approximately 6in (15cm) apart on both sides of the bag. Pin in place. Sew the strap down along the bottom of the bag and 10in (25cm) up from the bottom on all four sides of the strap.

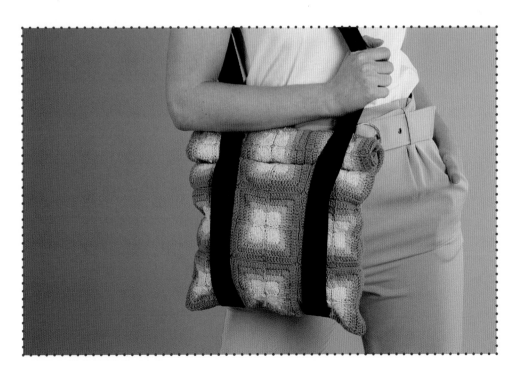

TWEED BAG

DESIGNED BY AMY PARKER

Small yet perfectly formed, this classic bag is ideal for beginners to make. It's a great way to practise a stitch that gives a professional finish. You will also learn how to attach a zip and sew together a project with ease.

SKILL LEVEL: EASY

YOU'LL NEED

YARN

No. 3 lightweight yarn
(shown in Rowan Felted Tweed DK)
A – 1 x 50g Lotus Leaf 205
B – 1 x 50g Phantom 153

HOOK

3.5mm (US E/4)

HABERDASHERY

1 x ½in (11mm) zip
2 x ½in (11mm) D-rings
2 x ½in (11mm) swivel clips or bag clips with
    a D-ring end
2 x stitch markers (clip style)
Large-eyed sewing needle

TWEED BAG

SIZE
Body: Approximately 10in (25cm) wide × 12in (30cm) high.
Handle/strap: Approximately ½in (11mm) wide × 32in (81cm) long.

TENSION
23sts and 21 rows to 4in (10cm), measured over pattern stitch using a 3.5mm (US E/4) hook, after blocking (see page 14).

METHOD
SIDE 1
Using 3.5mm hook and yarn A, make 58ch.
Row 1: 1dc into 2nd ch from hook, *1ch, miss 1ch, 1dc into the next ch; repeat from * to the end, ending with 1dc into final ch, turn. 29dc.
Row 2: 2ch, miss 1dc, 1dc into ch-sp, 1ch, miss 1dc, *1dc into ch-sp, ch1, miss 1dc; repeat from * until 2dc remain, 1dc into remaining ch-sp, 1ch, 1dc into the top of the final dc, turn.

Row 3: 2ch, miss 1dc, 1dc into ch-sp, 1ch, miss 1dc, *1dc into ch-sp, ch1, miss 1dc; repeat from * until 1dc remains, 1dc into ch-sp between the final dc and the end, turn.
Repeat Row 3 until you have a total of 63 rows.
Fasten off.

SIDE 2
Work same as Side 1 using yarn B.

HANDLE
Using the 3.5mm hook and yarn B, make 10ch.
Follow Rows 1–3 for the main body, until the handle measures 32in (81cm) or desired length plus 1in (2.5cm).
Fasten off.
Cut a length of yarn twice the length of the handle and thread it through the darning needle. Fold the handle in half with the RS facing out. Using mattress stitch (see page 25), sew up the open side of the handle.

MAKING UP

Press the main body, as described in Crochet Basics (see page 14).

Press the handle, ensuring it is 32in (81cm) long or your required length. Press with the seamed side facing down.

With the RS facing each other (WS facing out), sew the sides together, leaving the top open. Turn the bag RS out.

With yarn A, back stitch along one side of the zip. With yarn B, back stitch along the other side of the zip.

Place the zip inside the bag with the colours matching. ss the zip to the bag, one side at a time, using the matching yarn and working through one stitch of the bag and one back stitch on the zip.

D-RING TAB (MAKE 2)

Using a 3.5mm hook and yarn B, make 4ch.
Row 1: 1dc into 2nd ch from hook, 1ch, miss 1ch, 1dc into next ch, turn.
Row 2: 2ch, miss first dc, 1dc into ch-sp, 1ch, 1dc into top of last dc, turn.
Row 3: 2ch, miss first dc, 1dc into ch-sp, 1ch, miss 1dc, 1dc into ch-sp between the last dc and the end of the row.

Repeat Row 3 once more. Fasten off, leaving a long tail.

Place the stitch marker on the side seam of the bag 6½in (16cm) from the bottom on each side of the yarn B side of the bag.

Thread the D-ring tabs through the D-rings. Fold the tab in half and, using the long tail, sew the tab closed. Do not cut the long tail yet.

Centre the D-ring tabs to the markers and sew as close to the seam as possible without going onto yarn A.

Thread 1in (2.5cm) of each end of the handle through the D-ring clips. Sew WS together securely.
Attach the clips to the D-rings on the bag and fold your bag in half.

> **Tip**
> Try swapping over the colours and making the main body of the bag in brown and the other parts in green.

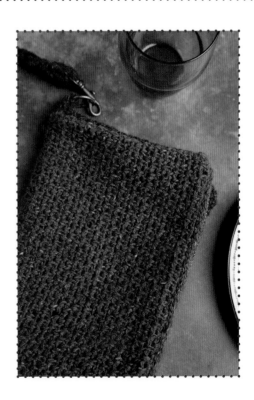

BACKPACK

DESIGNED BY EMMA OSMOND

This sturdy backpack is worked holding two strands of yarn together to create a durable, dense fabric. With details such as double straps, a drawstring fastening and a flap for security, this hard-working bag is ideal for the office, days out or shopping trips.

SKILL LEVEL: INTERMEDIATE

YOU'LL NEED

YARN

No. 1 super fine yarn
(shown in Anchor Creativa Fino 4ply)
A – 16 x 50g Col. 0434
B – 1 x 50g Col. 0152

HOOK

3.5mm (US E/4)

HABERDASHERY

2 x stitch markers
Large-eyed tapestry needle

BACKPACK

SIZE
Approximately 27½in (70cm) wide x 16¾in (43cm) high.

TENSION
17sts and 8 rows to 4in (10cm), measured over treble crochet using the 3.5mm hook and using 1 strand each of yarn A and yarn B held together.

METHOD
BASE
Pattern note – The base is worked in a spiral. Use a stitch marker to mark the beginning of the rounds and move it up after each round.
Using the 3.5mm (US E4) hook and 1 strand each of yarn A and yarn B held together, make 38ch.

Round 1: 1tr into 2nd ch from hook, 1tr into the next 35ch, 3tr into the next ch, 1tr into the next 35ch, 2tr into the last ch. 76sts.

Round 2: 2tr into the next st, 1tr into next 35sts, 2tr into next 3sts, 1tr into next 35sts, 2tr into the next 2sts. 82sts.

Round 3: 2tr into next st, 1tr into next 36sts, (2tr into next st, 1tr into foll st) 3 times, 1tr into next 35sts, (2tr into next st, 1tr into foll st) twice. 88sts.

Round 4: 1tr into next 2sts, 2tr into next st, 1tr into next 35sts, (1tr into next 2sts, 2tr into foll st) 3 times, 1tr into next 35sts, (1tr into next 2sts, 2tr into foll st) twice. 94sts.

Round 5: 1tr into next st, 2tr into next st, 1tr into next 38sts, (2tr into next st, 1tr into foll 3sts) 3 times, 1tr into next 35sts, 2tr into next st, 1tr into next 3sts, 2tr into next st, 1tr into next 2sts. 100sts.

Round 6: 1tr into next 4sts, 2tr into next st, 1tr into next 35sts, (1tr into next 4sts, 2tr into foll st) 3 times, 1tr into next 35sts, (1tr into the next 4sts, 2tr in the next st) twice. 106sts.

Round 7: 1tr into next st, 2tr into next st, 1tr into next 41sts, 2tr into next st, 1tr into next

5sts, 2tr into next st, 1tr into next 4sts, 2tr into next st, 1tr into next 41sts, 2tr into next st, 1tr into next 5sts, 2tr into next st, 1tr into next 3sts. 112sts.

Round 8: 1tr into next 6sts, 2tr into next st, 1tr into next 35sts, (1tr in next 6sts, 2tr into foll st) 3 times, 1tr in next 35sts, (1tr into next 6sts, 2tr in next st) twice. 118sts.
Join with a ss.

BODY

Round 1: 1ch, 1tr through the back loop only into the next 118sts.

Round 2: 1tr into each st to the end.

Round 3: Repeat Round 2 for a further 37 rounds.
Fasten off.

FLAP

Using the 3.5mm (US E4) hook and 1 strand each of yarn A and yarn B held together, make 50ch.

Row 1: 1tr into 2nd chain from hook, 1tr into next 47ch, turn. 48sts.

Row 2: 2ch (do not count as st), 1tr into each st to the end, turn. 48sts.
Repeat Row 2 a further 15 times.

Row 18: 2ch (do not count as st), 1tr, tr2tog, 1tr into each st to last 3sts, tr2tog, 1tr, turn. 46sts.

Row 19: Repeat Row 18 until 20sts remain.
Fasten off.
Place a stitch marker in the middle of the foundation row.

FLAP BORDER

Using the 3.5mm hook and 1 strand each of yarn A and yarn B held together, rejoin the yarn to the side of Row 1.

Row 1: 2ch (do not count as st), 1tr into base of beg ch, work 1tr into each of the next 30 row ends, work 2tr into the corner st, 1tr into the next 18sts along the bottom of the flap, work 2tr into the corner st, 1tr into each of the next 31 row ends. 84sts.
Fasten off.

STRAP (MAKE 2)

Using the 3.5mm (US E4) hook and holding two strands together, make 138ch.

Row 1: 1tr into 2nd ch from hook, 1tr into each ch to the end, turn. 136sts.

Row 2: 2ch (do not count as st), 1tr into each st to the end, turn.
Repeat Row 2 a further four times. Fasten off.

MAKING UP

Place a stitch marker in the centre back of the backpack. Pin the middle of each strap to the marker.

With the WS facing out and using a back stitch, sew the flap to the bag, encasing the two bag straps.

Using a back stitch (see page 25), attach the other ends of the straps to the base of the bag, approximately
2in (5cm) in from the side of the bag.

(continued overleaf)

DRAWSTRING

Cut eight lengths of yarn A and B 4½yd (4m) long and tie a knot at each end.

Secure one end and twist the other end until the cord starts to twist around itself.

Take the centre of the cord with your free hand so that it twists from the middle and continue to twist the cord until its entire length has a firm twist.

Holding the knot at each end of the length together, knot again approximately 4in (10cm) up from the original knots to join.

Make a knot in the other end approximately 4½in (12cm) from the end. Trim both ends to match.

Using a large tapestry needle, weave one end through the top of the backpack to create a drawstring.

YOGA MAT BAG

DESIGNED BY EMMA OSMOND

Worked in a 100 per cent cotton yarn, this yoga mat bag has a repeated treble crochet pattern. The length of the bag and the length of the straps can be adjusted easily. This bag is a quick weekend project to make for yourself or a friend.

SKILL LEVEL: INTERMEDIATE

YOU'LL NEED

YARN

No. 3 lightweight cotton yarn
(shown in Rowan Handknit Cotton)
3 x 50g Ice Winter 239

HOOK

4.5mm (US 7)

HABERDASHERY

Sharp scissors
2 x stitch markers
Large-eyed sewing needle

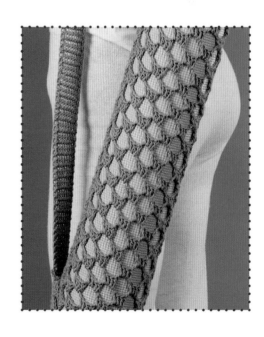

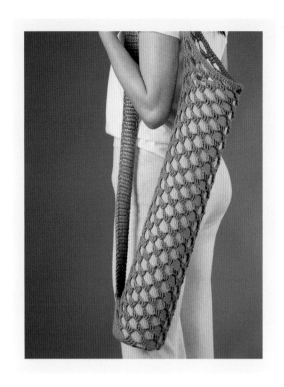

YOGA MAT BAG

SIZE
5½in (13cm) circumference × 21½in (55cm) high.

TENSION
20sts and 20 rows to 4in (10cm), measured over double crochet using a 4.5mm hook.
20sts and 6 rounds to 4in (10cm), measured over pattern using a 4.5mm hook.

METHOD
SPECIAL INSTRUCTIONS
Adjustable loop – wrap the yarn around your index finger, over the top of the finger anticlockwise and all the way around the finger. Slide the loop off your finger and work the sts for the first round into this loop. Pull tightly closed and ss into the 1st st.

BASE
With the 4.5mm hook, make an adjustable loop (see Special Instructions, left) and work 6dc into the loop.

Round 1: 2dc into each st, join with a ss. 12sts.
Round 2: *2dc into next st, 1dc into foll st; rep from * to end, join with ss. 18sts.
Round 3: *2dc into next st, 1dc into foll 2sts; rep from * to end, join with ss. 24sts.
Round 4: *2dc into next st, 1dc into foll 3sts; rep from * to end, join with ss. 30sts.
Round 5: *2dc into next st, 1dc into foll 4sts; rep from * to end, join with ss. 36sts.
Round 6: *2dc into next st, 1dc into foll 5sts; rep from * to end, join with ss. 42sts.
Round 7: *2dc into next st, 1dc into foll 6sts; rep from * to end, join with ss. 48sts.
Round 8: *2dc into next st, 1dc into foll 7sts; rep from * to end, join with ss. 54sts.
Round 9: *2dc into next st, 1dc into foll 8sts; rep from * to end, join with ss. 60sts.
Round 10: *2dc into next st, 1dc into foll 9sts; rep from * to end, join with ss. 66sts.

Round 11: *2dc into next st, 1dc into foll 10sts, rep from * to the end, join with ss. 72sts.

BAG

Round 1: 1ch, 1dc into the back of each st to the end of the round. 72sts.
Place one stitch marker at the end of the row and a 2nd marker 8sts before this.
Round 2: 6ch (counts as 1tr and 4ch), *miss 4sts, 1tr into next and 3 foll sts, 4ch; rep from * 7 times more, miss 4sts, 1tr into next 3sts, join with a ss into 2nd ch.
Round 3: 1ss into ch-sp, 2ch (this counts as a tr), 3tr into same ch-sp, * 4ch, 4tr into foll ch-sp; rep from * 7 times more, 4ch, join with a ss into 2nd ch.
Round 4: 6ch (counts as 1tr and 4ch), *4tr into ch-sp, 4ch; rep from * 7 times more, 4tr into last ch-sp, join with a ss into 2nd ch.
Repeat the last two rounds until the bag measures 21½in (55cm), ending on Round 2.
Round 5: 1ch, *4dc into ch-sp, 1dc into top of each tr; repeat from * 7 times more, 4dc into next ch-sp, 1dc into the top of the last 3tr, 1dc into top of ch, join with a ss.
Round 6: 1ch, 1dc into each st to the end of the round.

STRAP

Row 1 (WS): 1ch, 1dc into next 8sts, turn.
Row 2 (RS): 1ch, 1dc into next 8sts, turn.
Repeat the last 2 rows until the strap measures 23½in (60cm) long, ending with a WS row. Fasten off.

MAKING UP

Attach the strap to the base of the bag with the RS of the strap facing, using the stitch markers as a guide. Sew the strap to the base of the bag using any spare yarn and back stitch. Using a 4.5mm hook, work 99dc across the long side edge of the handle, work other side to match. Using a 4.5mm hook, work 99dc across the long side edge of the handle, work other side to match.

APPLIQUÉ CIRCLES BAG

DESIGNED BY KATHY MERRICK

This design incorporates eye-catching decoration using applique circles in different sizes. The circles are fun to create and add texture and colour to a basic tote bag. Choose colours that blend for a sophisticated look.

SKILL LEVEL: REQUIRES EXPERIENCE

YOU'LL NEED

YARN

No. 3 lightweight yarn
(shown in Rowan Felted Tweed DK)
A – 3 x 50g Duck Egg 173
B – 3 x 50g Celadon 184

HOOK

3.25mm (US D/3)

HABERDASHERY

4 x ¾in (4.2cm) buttons (flat with holes,
    not shanks)
Large-eyed darning needle

APPLIQUÉ CIRCLES BAG

SIZE:
Front and back panels: Approximately 16in (40cm) wide × 14½in (37cm) high.

TENSION
18sts and 16 rows to 4in (10cm), measured over half treble crochet using the 3.25mm hook.

METHOD
SPECIAL INSTRUCTIONS
When changing colour, be sure to work the last step of the stitch in the new colour.

Always keep the colour not in use on the wrong side.

Adjustable loop (beginning of motif) – wrap the yarn around your index finger, over the top of the finger anticlockwise and all the way around the finger. Slide the loop off your finger and work the sts for the first round into this loop. Pull tightly closed and ss into 1st st.

FRONT AND BACK PANELS (MAKE 2)
Using the 3.25mm hook and yarn A, make 74ch.
Row 1: 1htr into 3rd ch from hook, 1htr into next 35ch, changing to yarn B in 36th st; work 36htr in yarn B, turn. 72sts.
Row 2: 2ch, 1htr into next 36sts, changing to A in the last st and working rem sts in yarn A. Work 15 more rows, changing colour at the centre.
Row 3: Work the entire row in yarn B. Now work 17 rows with the colours at the opposite ends from the first section, switching at the centre of the row.
Row 4: Work the entire row in yarn A. Now work 17 rows with the colours as for the first section.
Fasten off.

SIDE PANEL
Using the 3.25mm hook and yarn A, make 182ch.
Row 1: 1htr into the 3rd ch from the hook and into each ch to the end, turn.
Row 2: 2ch, htr into each st.

Change to yarn B.

Repeat Row 2 twice. Continue as set, working 2 rows of each colour until there are 18 rows. Carry the colour not in use up the side of the panel.

Fasten off.

LARGE MOTIF (MAKE 3 in yarn A, MAKE 2 in yarn B)

Round 1: Make an adjustable loop (see Special Instructions, left) and 12htc into the loop.

Round 2: 4ch (counts as 1st dtr), work dtr into the same st; 2dtr into each st; ss into first st of the round. 24sts.

Round 3: 1ch, work 1dc into each st; ss to the 1st st of the round.

Round 4: As for Round 2. 48sts.

Round 5: As for Round 3. Fasten off, leaving a 12in (30cm) tail for sewing to the front panel.

SMALL MOTIF (MAKE 2 in yarn A, MAKE 3 in yarn B)

Work as for the large motif, ending after Round 3. Leave tails for sewing to the front panel. Set aside one large motif in yarn A and one in yarn B to attach to the handle.

HANDLES (MAKE 2)

With 1 strand each of yarn A and yarn B held together, make 141ch.

Row 1: 1ss into each ch across, turn. 140sts.

Row 2: 1ch, ss into the back loop of each st.

Row 3: 1ch, work as for Row 2.

Fasten off, leaving a 12in (30cm) tail for sewing.

MAKING UP

Press as described in Crochet Basics (see page 14).

Sew the motifs to the front panel. Thread a tail from the motif into a darning needle. Using the photo on page 72 as a guide, sew the motif to the panel, working into one st of the motif

edge and out through the next until all sts are attached.

With the wrong sides of the panels together, beginning at the right side of the front panel, dc into the edges by joining one st of the side panel to one row of the front, then one st of the side panel to one st of the bottom edge, then one st of the side panel to one row of the remaining front edge. Repeat with the back panel.

With the wrong sides together, ss two large motifs together. Make 30ch, ss to the motif, next to the beginning ch.

Sew in all the tails. Slip ch the loop of the sewn-together large motif around one end of one handle.

Place one end of the handle with motif 1in (2.5cm) from the top edge of the front and 2in (5cm) from the side edge. Place a button on top of the handle and sew through the button, handle and bag, making sure the handle is secure. Repeat for the other end and then again for the back handle.

Block (see page 14) as necessary to the finished measurements.

CROSS-BODY DRAWSTRING BAG

DESIGNED BY LOUISE BOLLANOS

A cross-body bag that is large enough to hold your essentials while you are on the go. This pattern is great for anyone who has some experience of crochet. Add tassels or a chain strap to customize your bag, and wear it with your go-to outfits all year round!

SKILL LEVEL: REQUIRES EXPERIENCE

YOU'LL NEED

YARN

No. 5 bulky weight yarn
(shown in Paintbox Yarns Simply Chunky)
2 x 100g Soft Fudge 309

HOOK

6mm (US J/10)

HABERDASHERY

39in (1m) of cord for drawstring
Beads, thread, cord as desired to
    embellish tassel
39in (99cm) metal chain (optional)
3 x 1in (2.5cm) key ring clip to attach tassel and
    strap to bag
2 x metal rings
8in (21cm) long piece of card to make the tassel
1 x stitch marker

CROSS-BODY DRAWSTRING BAG

SIZE
6½in (16.5cm) diameter x 9in (23cm) high.

TENSION
12sts and 10 rows to 4in (10cm), measured over double crochet using a 6mm hook.

METHOD
SPECIAL INSTRUCTIONS
When working the base, make 3ch at the beginning of each round, which counts as one tr. The base is worked in a spiral, with the RS always facing out.

Place a marker on the last st and move it up after each round to keep track of the stitch count.

Pattern note – you can substitute a crochet strap for a chain, as detailed in the pattern.

BASE
Using the 6mm hook, make 3ch, join with ss to the 3rd ch to form a ring.

Round 1: 3ch, 11tr into the centre of the ring, join with ss to the top of the first 3ch, place marker. 12sts.

Round 2: 3ch (counts as 1tr), tr into next stitch, 3tr into each of the next 3sts, 1tr into the next 3sts, 3tr into each of the next 3sts, 1tr into the last stitch, join with ss to top of first 3ch. 24sts.

Round 3: 3ch, 1tr into each of the next 2sts, 3tr into next st, 1dtr into next 2sts, 3tr in next st, 1dtr into next 2sts, 3tr into next st, 1tr into next 5sts, 3tr into the next st, 1dtr into next 2sts, 3tr into next st, 1dtr into next 2sts, 3tr into next st, 1tr into last 2sts, join with ss to top of first 3ch of round. 36sts.

Round 4: 3ch, 1tr into next 3sts, 3tr into the next st, 1dtr into next 4sts, 3tr into the next st, 1dtr into next 4sts, 3tr into next st, 1tr into next 7sts, 3tr into next st, 1dtr into next 4sts, 3tr into next st 1dtr into next 4sts. 3tr into the next st 1tr into the last 3sts. join with ss to the top of the first 3ch of the round. 48sts.

Round 5: 3ch, 1tr into next 4sts, 3tr into the next st, 1dtr into next 6sts, 3tr into next st, 1dtr into next 6sts, 3tr into next st, 1tr into next 9sts, 3tr into next st, 1dtr into next 6sts, 3tr into next st, 1dtr into next 6sts, 3tr into next st, 1tr into last 4sts, join with ss to the top of the first 3ch of the round. 60sts.
Round 6: 1dc into the back loop only of each st.

BAG

Round 7: 1ch, 1dc in each st, join with ss. Repeat Round 7 until the bag measures 9in (23cm). Fasten off.

CROCHET BAG STRAP

With the 6mm hook, make 156ch.
Row 1: 1dc into 2nd ch from the hook and every ch in the row, turn.
Row 2: 1ch, 1dc into each st. Fasten off.
Fold each end over a metal ring and sew closed.

MAKING UP

Weave the drawstring cord approximately 1½in (4cm) below the top edge through every 3rd st.

STRAPS

Attach the strap or chain to each side of the bag using the key ring clips.

TASSEL

Wrap the yarn approximately 30 times around the 8in (21cm) length of card. Slip the tassel from the card and wrap tightly with a separate strand of yarn or decorative thread approximately 1in (3cm) from the top. Cut the bottom of the tassel open and trim evenly. Embellish with beads or charms. Attach to the bag with a key ring clip.

Tip
This bag can be made in any colour with decorative items added, such as tassels and bag charms. You can also make it in different fibres, such as cotton or raffia for the warmer months.

CROSS-BODY PHONE WALLET

DESIGNED BY LOUISE BOLLANOS

Wearing this cross-body phone wallet means that your phone can be accessed at all times. An easy pattern for absolute beginners, the neat design uses basic techniques and is quick to work. Adapt the size to your phone and make a few wallets as gifts for friends.

SKILL LEVEL: EASY

YOU'LL NEED

YARN
No. 5 bulky weight yarn
(shown in Paintbox Yarns Simply Chunky)
1 x 100g in Light Caramel 308

HOOK
6mm (US J/10) hook

HABERDASHERY
43in (110cm) bag chain
2 x 1in (3cm) key ring clips for the bag chain
2 x 1in (3cm) rings to attach key ring clips
1 x 1in (3cm) magnetic fastening
Large-eyed sewing needle

CROSS-BODY PHONE WALLET

SIZE
4in (10cm) wide × 7in (18cm) long.
Strap: 43in (110cm).

TENSION
12sts and 10 rows to 4in (10cm), measured over double crochet using a 6mm hook.

METHOD
SPECIAL INSTRUCTIONS
The sample phone wallet fits an iPhone 11 Pro Max: 3in (8cm) × 6in (15cm).

Adjust the size for your phone by measuring the height and width, then making a chain to the width size, adding two extra chains not including the turning chain. Then, follow the pattern until you can fit your phone inside comfortably and fold over the top flap by at least 3in (8cm).

WALLET
Using the 6mm hook, make 12ch, turn.
Row 1: 1ch, 1dc into every ch, turn.
Row 2: 1ch, 1dc into every st, turn.
Repeat Row 2 until the piece is 18in (46cm) or the desired length.
Fasten off.

MAKING UP
FASTENING INSERT (MAKE 2)
With the 6mm hook, make 5ch, turn.

Row 1: 1ch, 1dc into every ch, ch 1, turn.
Row 2: 1ch, 1dc into each st, turn.
Rep Row 2 twice more. The piece measures approximately 1½in (4cm).
Fasten off.

STRAP
Use a length of chain that is 43in (110cm) and attach it with two key ring clips, or crochet a strap and attach it with two rings and two key ring clips.

CROCHET STRAP

With the 6mm hook, make 125ch, turn.

Row 1: 1ch, 1dc into every ch, turn.
Row 2: 1ch, 1dc into every st, turn.
Fasten off.

Fold down the end of the crochet strap 1in (3cm), place a key ring clip in the fold and sew it down. Repeat for the opposite end. Sew the strap to both sides of the wallet.

Attach the fastening to the inserts. Sew or dc one insert to the inside of the lower end of the wallet approximately 1in (3cm) from the edge. Sew or dc 2nd insert 1in (3cm) from the edge on the top of the piece. This will be the fold-over flap.

Fold the bottom flap over, with the right sides facing, and sew or dc the seam for 7in (18cm) on each side.

Turn the right sides out and attach the strap to the wallet using one clip on each side of the bag. Place your phone inside, folding over the top flap to close.

Tip
This speedy project is great for using up yarn in your stash. Add a tassel charm or fringing to the fold-over flap for extra decoration.

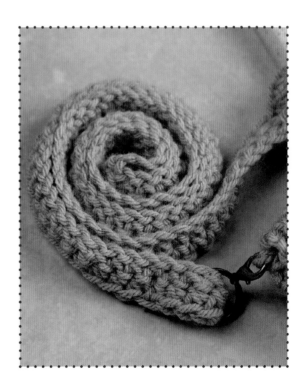

SLOUCHY SHOULDER BAG

DESIGNED BY LOUISE BOLLANOS

This slouchy shoulder bag has enough capacity to carry your essentials, plus a few extras. The handles are comfortable to wear over your shoulder on long trips and the roomy bag is sturdy enough to carry whatever you need.

SKILL LEVEL: EASY

YOU'LL NEED

YARN

No. 5 bulky weight yarn
(shown in Paintbox Yarns Simply Chunky)
1 x 100g Light Caramel 308

HOOK

6mm (US J/10) hook

HABERDASHERY

43in (110cm) bag chain
2 x 1in (3cm) key ring clips for the bag chain
2 x 1in (3cm) rings to attach key ring clips
1 x 1in (3cm) magnetic fastening
2 x Stitch markers

SLOUCHY SHOULDER BAG

SIZE
12in (30cm) diameter of base x 14in (36cm) high.

TENSION
12sts and 10 rows to 4in (10cm), measured over double crochet using a 6mm hook.

METHOD
SPECIAL INSTRUCTIONS
The bag is worked in the round, in a continuous spiral with the RS always facing out. Do not turn at the end of each round. Place a stitch marker and move it up at the end of each round to keep count of the sts.

BASE
Using the 6mm hook, make 4ch and join with a ss in the first ch to form a ring.
Round 1 (RS): 1ch; 8dc in ring. 8sts.
Round 2: 2dc into each dc. 16sts.
Round 3: *1dc into next dc, 2dc into next dc; repeat from * to end. 24sts.
Round 4: 1dc into each dc.

Round 5: *1dc into next dc, 2dc into next dc; repeat from * to end. 36sts.
Round 6: 1dc into each dc.
Round 7: *1dc into each of next 2dc, 2dc into next dc; repeat from * to end. 48sts.
Round 8: 1dc into each dc.
Round 9: *1dc into each of next 3dc, 2dc into next dc; repeat from * to end. 60sts.
Round 10: 1dc into each dc.
Round 11: 1dc into each of first 2dc, 2dc in next dc, *1dc into each of next 4dc, 2dc into next dc; repeat from * ending with 1dc into each of the last 2dc. 72sts.
Round 12: 1dc into each dc.
Round 13: 1dc into each of first 2dc, 2dc into next dc, *1dc into each of the next 5dc, 2dc into next dc; repeat from * ending with 1dc into each of the last 3dc. 84sts.
Round 14: 1dc into each dc.
Round 15: 1dc into each of first 2dc, 2dc into next dc, *1dc into each of next 6dc, 2dc into next dc; repeat from * ending with 1dc into each of last 4dc. 96sts.

Round 16: 1dc into each dc.

Round 17: 1dc into each of first 2dc, 2dc into the next dc, *1dc into each of next 7dc, 2dc into the next dc; repeat from * ending with 1dc into each of the last 5dc. 108sts.

Round 18: 1dc into each dc.

Round 19: 1dc into each of first 2dc, 2dc into next dc, *1dc into each of next 8dc, 2dc into next dc* repeat from * ending with 1dc into each of last 6dc. 120sts.

Round 20: 1dc into each dc. Place a new marker at end of the round.

BAG

Keep moving the first marker up to mark the beginning of rounds and keep the second marker in place to count the rounds.

Rounds 21–50: 120dc around.

STRAPS

Round 51: 1dc into next 15sts, 55ch, miss next 30sts for first strap, dc into the next 30sts, 55ch, miss the next 30sts for second strap, dc into last 15 sts. 170sts.

Round 52: 1dc into each dc and ch.

Repeat the previous round 3 more times.

Fasten off.

DRAWSTRING STORAGE BAG

DESIGNED BY LOUISE BOLLANOS

Using only double crochet stitches, you can create this pretty drawstring bag in a choice of two designs. The first is a colour block design that is ideal for beginners. The second bag is worked in a chevron stitch pattern, which will introduce you to an easy but intricate-looking design, using treble crochet stitches.

SKILL LEVEL: EASY

YOU'LL NEED

YARN

No. 5 bulky weight yarn
(shown in Paintbox Yarns Simply Chunky)
1 x 100g Light Caramel 308

Colour Block Bag
A – 1 x 100g Candyfloss Pink 349
B – 1 x 100g Stormy Grey 304
C – 1 x 100g Bubblegum Pink 350

Chevron Stripes Bag
A – 1 x 100g Candyfloss Pink 349
B – 1 x 100g Stormy Grey 304
C – 1 x 100g Bubblegum Pink 350

HOOK
6mm (US J/10) hook

HABERDASHERY
Large-eyed darning needle

DRAWSTRING STORAGE BAG

COLOUR BLOCK BAG
SIZE
Before seaming: 36in (92cm) high × 17in (43cm) wide.
Length folded and seamed: 18in (46cm).

CHEVRON BAG
SIZE
Before seaming: 36in (92cm) high × 17in (43cm) wide.
Length folded and seamed: 18in (46cm).

TENSION
Colour Block
12sts and 10 rows to 4in (10cm), measured over double crochet using a 6mm hook.

Chevron
12sts and 6 rows to 4in (10cm), measured over treble crochet using a 6mm hook.

METHOD
SPECIAL INSTRUCTIONS
The bags are both made in one long piece, folded in half and seamed.

COLOUR BLOCK BAG
With the 6mm hook and yarn C, make 50ch, ch 1, turn.
Row 1 (RS): 1dc into 2nd ch from hook, 1dc into each ch to end, turn.
Row 2: 1ch (do not count as st), 1dc into each st to end, turn.
Repeat Row 2 until the work measures 4in (10cm), ending with a WS row.
Change to yarn B.
Work as established for 3in (8cm) more.
Change to yarn A.
Work as established for 25½in (65cm) more.
Change to yarn B.
Work as established for 3in (8cm) more.
Change to yarn C.
Work as established for 4in (10cm) more.
Fasten off.

MAKING UP
With the RS facing out, fold in half. Using the matching yarn for each colour block section, dc the sides together to form a bag. Turn the bag right side out.

DRAWSTRING CORD
With yarn B, ch162sts and fasten off, leaving a tail of yarn approx 4in (10cm) long. Thread the tail through the darning needle and feed the chain through the dc gaps approximately 1½in (4cm) from the top edge of the bag, beginning and ending at the centre front. Knot the cord at each end and weave in any loose ends.

CHEVRON STRIPES BAG
Using the 6mm hook and yarn A, make 51ch, turn.

Row 1 (RS): 2tr into 2nd ch from hook, *1tr into each of the next 7ch, miss next ch, 1tr into each of the next 7ch, 3tr in next ch; repeat from * to end, working 2tr in the last ch, turn.

Row 2: With yarn A, 1 ch, 2tr in first tr, *1tr into each of the next 7tr, miss next 2tr, 1tr into each of the next 7tr, 3tr into next tr, repeat from * to end, working 2tr into the last tr, turn.

Rows 3 and 4: Change to yarn B and repeat Row 2 twice.

Rows 5 and 6: Change to yarn C and repeat Row 2 twice.

Rows 7 and 8: Change to yarn A and repeat Row 2 twice.

Rows 3–8 form the pattern.
Repeat the pattern seven times more.
Change to yarn A.
Repeat Rows 3 and 4 once more.
Fasten off.

MAKING UP
With the RS facing out, fold in half. Using yarn A, dc the sides together to form a bag, leaving the top edge open for approximately 1in (2.5cm) on each side. Turn the bag right side out.

DRAWSTRING CORD
With yarn B and the 6mm hook, make ch162sts and fasten off, leaving a tail of yarn approximately 4in (10cm) long.

Thread the tail through the darning needle and feed the chain through the tr gaps approximately 1½in (4cm) from the top edge of the bag, beginning and ending at the centre front.

LEOPARD PRINT POUCH

DESIGNED BY EMMA WRIGHT

Here's a pouch with a punch. In an adorable leopard print, this handy little pouch is the perfect make-up bag or wallet to slip inside your handbag. It's also an exciting way to practise combining colours to create a striking effect.

SKILL LEVEL: INTERMEDIATE

YOU'LL NEED

YARN
No. 3 lightweight yarn
(shown in KPC Yarn DK)
A – 2 x 50g Inca

No. 3 lightweight yarn
(shown in Rowan Creative Linen)
B – 1 x 100g Stormy 635

No. 3 lightweight yarn
(shown in Erika Knight Studio Linen)
C – 1 x 50g Milk 400

HOOK
4mm (US G/6)

HABERDASHERY
1 x 11in (28cm) zip
Large-eyed sewing needle

LEOPARD PRINT POUCH

SIZE
12in (30cm) wide × 9in (23cm) high.

TENSION
18sts × 10 rows to 4in (10cm), measured over double crochet using a 4mm hook.

METHOD
SPECIAL INSTRUCTIONS

Pattern note – when a new colour is introduced, lay the other colours over the hook, towards the back of the work, and trap inside each dc worked to trail non-used yarns across the row. Then, when needed, pick up the new colour and lay the old colour behind, as you did previously.

SIDES (MAKE 2)

Using the 4mm hook and yarn A, make 56ch. Place the chart patt (see page 96), working first st from the chart in yarn A into 2nd ch from the hook and adding yarn B and yarn C where stated as follows:

Row 1 (RS): 11dc in yarn A, 2dc in B, 8dc in yarn A, 4dc in yarn B, 10dc in yarn A, 2dc in yarn B, 5dc in yarn A, 1dc in yarn B, 2dc in yarn C, 1dc in yarn B, 3dc in yarn A, 2dc in yarn B, 4dc in yarn C, turn. 55sts.

Row 2: 1ch, 3dc in yarn C, 3dc in yarn A, 4dc in yarn A, 2dc in B, 5dc in yarn A, 2dc in yarn B, 2dc in yarn C, 20dc in yarn A, 2dc in yarn C, 1dc in yarn B, 11dc in yarn A, turn.

Row 3: 1ch, 3dc in yarn A, 2dc in yarn B, 4dc in yarn A, 1dc in yarn B, 5dc in yarn C, 17dc in yarn A, 5dc in yarn C, 2dc in yarn B, 11dc in yarn A, 2dc in yarn B, 3dc in yarn C, turn.

Row 4: 1ch, 2dc in yarn C, 2dc in yarn B, 12dc in yarn A, 3dc in yarn B, 4dc in yarn C, 1dc in yarn B, 16dc in yarn A, 3dc in yarn C, 1dc in yarn B, 5dc in yarn A, 2dc in yarn C, 1dc in yarn B, 3dc in yarn A, turn.

Row 5: 1ch, dc5 in yarn A, dc2 in yarn C, dc14 in yarn A, dc2 in yarn B, dc9 in yarn A, dc2 in yarn B, dc5 in yarn C, dc14 in yarn A, dc1 in yarn B, dc1 in yarn C, dc1 in yarn B, turn.

Row 6: 1ch, 1dc in yarn B, 16dc in yarn A, 1dc in yarn B, 4dc in yarn C, 2dc in yarn B, 6dc in yarn A, 5dc in B, 8dc in yarn A, 2dc in yarn B, 1 dc in yarn C, 4dc in yarn A.

Row 7: 1ch, 9dc in yarn A, 2dc in yarn C, 1dc in yarn B, 6dc in yarn A, 3dc in yarn B, 3dc in yarn C, 8dc in yarn A, 2dc in yarn B, 2dc in yarn C, 2dc in yarn B, 2dc in yarn A, 2dc in yarn B, 12dc in yarn A, 1dc in yarn B, turn.

Row 8: 1ch, 5dc in yarn A, 2dc in yarn B, 6dc in yarn A, 1dc in yarn B, 2dc in yarn C, 4dc in yarn A, 2dc in yarn B, 7dc in yarn A, 2dc in yarn B, 4dc in yarn C, 2dc in yarn B, 5dc in yarn A, 1dc in yarn B, 4dc in yarn C, 7dc in yarn A, 1dc in yarn B, turn.

Row 9: 1ch, 2dc in yarn B, 6dc in yarn A, 1dc in yarn B, 4dc in yarn C, 5dc in yarn A, 1dc in yarn B, 6dc in yarn C, 1dc in yarn B, 12dc in yarn A, 4dc in yarn C, 1dc in yarn B, 4dc in yarn A, 2dc in yarn C, 1dc in yarn B, 5dc in yarn A, turn.

Row 10: 1ch, 5dc in yarn A, 1dc in yarn B, 3dc in yarn C, 3dc in yarn A, 4dc in yarn C, 1dc in yarn B, 12dc in yarn A, 2dc in yarn B, 4dc in yarn C, 2dc in yarn B, 6dc in yarn A, 2dc in yarn C, 2dc in yarn B, 5dc in yarn A, 3dc in yarn C, turn.

These 10 rows set the chart pattern placement in dc. Continue working from the chart as set, completing Rows 11–22.

Row 23 (RS): 1ch, 1dc in every st.
Fasten off.

MAKING UP

With the zip open, insert it into the last row of each bag panel by placing the crochet fabric over the zip fabric and leaving the zip teeth exposed. Sew in place using yarn A and a running stitch (see Special Instructions, left). Fasten off the ends.

Using yarn A with the WS of the fabric together, join the sides and bottom of the bag with a dc going through both pieces of fabric.

SPECIAL INSTRUCTIONS

Running stitch – working from right to left, bring the needle up at A, go in at B and come back out at C. Continue in this manner, spacing stitches evenly. To end the stitch, go down through the fabric to the wrong side at B.

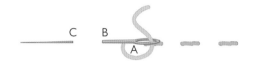

CHART

Key

A
B
C

MAKER'S PROJECT BAG

DESIGNED BY LOUISE BOLLANOS

With its interior pockets, this bag is perfect for storing your knitting or crochet makes and materials while you are on the go. The small strap means you can wear it on your wrist as you work, and the drawstring allows you to open and close the bag easily.

SKILL LEVEL: EASY

YOU'LL NEED

YARN

No. 5 bulky weight yarn
(shown in Paintbox Yarns Simply Chunky)
A – 2 x 100g Slate Grey 305
B – 1 x 100g Granite Grey 306
C – 1 x 100g Stormy Grey 304

HOOK

6mm (US J/10)

HABERDASHERY

Large-eyed darning needle

MAKER'S PROJECT BAG

SIZE
14in (36cm) wide × 9½in (24cm) high

TENSION
12sts and 10 rows to 4in (10cm), measured over double crochet using a 6mm hook.

METHOD
SPECIAL INSTRUCTIONS

The bag is made in 5 main pieces: a front panel, a back panel, 2 side panels and a base. These main pieces are joined together at the seams. The wrist strap and the drawstring cord are added later.

FRONT/BACK PANEL (MAKE 2)

Using the 6mm hook and yarn A, make 40ch, turn.

Row 1: 1dc into every ch, turn.

Row 2: 1ch, 1dc into every ch, turn.

Repeat Row 2 until the piece measures 10½in (27cm).

Fasten off.

BASE

Using the 6mm hook and yarn B, make 40ch, turn.

Row 1: 1dc into every ch, turn.

Row 2: 1ch, 1dc into every ch, turn.

Repeat Row 2 until the piece measures 5in (12cm).

Fasten off.

SIDE PANEL (MAKE 2)

Using the 6mm hook and yarn B, make 16ch.

Row 1: 1dc into every ch, turn.

Row 2: 1dc into 2nd st from the hook, 1dc in every st to the end of the row, turn.

Row 3: Repeat Row 2.

Rows 4 and 5: 1dc into every st, turn.

Rows 6 and 7: Repeat Row 2.

Repeat Rows 4–7 until 1st remains.

Fasten off.

INSERT

Using the 6mm hook and yarn B, make 36ch, turn.

Row 1: 1dc into every ch, turn.

Row 2: 1ch, 1dc into every st, turn.

Repeat Row 2 until the piece measures 5½in (14cm).

Fasten off.

WRIST STRAP

Using the 6mm hook and yarn A, make 20ch, turn.

Row 1: 1ch, 1dc into every ch, turn.

Row 2: 1ch, 1dc into every st, turn.

Repeat Row 2 once more.

Fasten off.

DRAWSTRING (MAKE 2)

Using the 6mm hook and yarn C, make 154ch. Fasten off, leaving a tail of 4in (10cm).

MAKING UP

Place the insert onto the front panel. Stitch into place using a mattress stitch (see page 25) or dc, attaching at the bottom edge and two sides, and leaving the top part of the panel open. Making sure sts are not visible on the RS of the front, with yarn C, create pockets for tools by stitching verticals into the insert and front panel.

Fold down the top of the front panel 1in (2.5cm) and tack to secure. Repeat on the back panel.

Working on the inside of the bag, with the WS facing you, seam the bottom edge of the front panel to the base. Repeat with the back panel.

Seam the bottom of the triangle side panel to one side of the base and then repeat on the other side.

Seam one of the triangle side panels to both the front and back panels. Then seam the remaining length of the panel, leaving the top folded edges open. Repeat on the other side.

Weave in all the loose ends and turn the right side out.

Using a darning needle, thread one drawstring through one end of the opening on the front panel, all the way through and out the other side, feeding it through the back panel to meet the other end. Do the same with the second drawstring through the opposite side of the bag. Two lengths of the cord hang at each side of the bag through each opening. Sew in the loose ends on the cords and then knot the two ties together. Pull the drawstrings to close the bag.

Sew the wrist strap to the front panel, just below the folded edge. Leave a 1in (2.5cm) gap and sew the other side of the wrist strap to the back panel just below the folded-over top edge.

> *Tip*
> This is a fabulous beginner project using basic stitches and techniques. If you like, you can add more pockets inside for your different tools and gadgets.

PICNIC BAG
DESIGNED BY EMMA OSMOND

With its top handles, this summery picnic bag is perfect for carrying snacks to keep you going on your outdoor adventures. Thanks to its stiff structure, this bag stands upright, ensuring that the contents won't fall out, and your picnic carrier always looks its best.

SKILL LEVEL: INTERMEDIATE

YOU'LL NEED

YARN
Anchor Creativa Fino
A – 2 x 50g of 00404
B – 3 x 50g of 00179

HOOK
3.5mm (US E/4) hook

HABERDASHERY
2 x stitch markers

PICNIC BAG

SIZE

Approximately 26½in (68cm) wide × 14½in (37cm) high.

TENSION

20sts and 11 rows to 4in (10cm), measured over double crochet holding 2 strands together using a 3.5mm hook.

METHOD

SPECIAL INSTRUCTIONS

Adjustable loop – wrap some yarn around your index finger, over the top of the finger anticlockwise and all the way around the finger. Slide the loop off your finger and work the sts for the first round into this loop. Pull tightly closed and ss into 1st st.

BASE

Using the 3.5mm hook and yarn A, and holding 2 strands together, make an adjustable loop (see Special Instructions, above).

Round 1: 6dc into loop.

Round 2: 2dc into each st. 12sts.

Round 3: *1dc into next st, 2dc into foll st; rep from * to end. 18sts.

Round 4: *1dc into next 2sts, 2dc into foll st; rep from * to end. 24sts.

Round 5: *1dc into next 3sts, 2dc into foll st; rep from * to end. 30sts.

Round 6: *1dc into next 4sts, 2dc into foll st; rep from * to end. 36sts.

Round 7: *1dc into next 5sts, 2dc into foll st; rep from * to end. 42sts.

Round 8: *1dc into next 6sts, 2dc into foll st; rep from * to end. 48sts.

Round 9: *1dc into next 7sts, 2dc into foll st; rep from * to end. 54sts.

Round 10: *1dc into next 8sts, 2dc into foll st; rep from * to end. 60sts.

Round 11: *1dc into next 9sts, 2dc into foll st; rep from * to end. 66sts.

Round 12: *1dc into next 10sts, 2dc into foll st; rep from * to end. Join with ss. 72sts.

SIDES

Round 1: Using yarn A, and holding 2 strands together, 1ch (do not count as st), 1dc into the back loop of each st to end. Join with a ss.

Round 2: 1ch (do not count as st), place marker on st just worked, 1dc into next 36sts, place a stitch marker on the last st worked, 1dc into each st to the end. Join with a ss.

Round 3: 1ch (do not count as st), 2dc into the next st, *1dc into each st until 1st before marker, work 2dc into next st**, 1dc into foll st, 2dc into next st, rep from * to ** once more. Join with a ss. 76sts.

Round 4: 1ch (do not count as st), 1dc into each st to end. Join with a ss.

Working inc as set by last 2 rounds, inc 1st before and after each stitch marker, making 4 extra stitches per 2-round repeat.

Round 5: Rep Rounds 3–4 a further 5 times. 96sts.

Change to yarn B, 2 strands held together.

Round 6: Rep Rounds 3–4 a further 10 times. 136sts.

Round 7: 1ch (do not count as st), work 1dc into each st to end.

Rep Round 7 until side measures 12½in (32cm).

HANDLES

Round 1: Using yarn B, and holding 2 strands together, 1ch (do not count as st), 1dc into foll 22sts, make 23ch, miss next 23sts, 1dc into next 46sts, make 23ch, miss next 23sts, work 1dc into next 23sts, join with a ss.

Round 2: 1ch (do not count as st), 1dc into next 22sts, work 23dc into ch-sp, 1dc into next 46sts, 23dc into ch-sp made on previous round, work 1dc into next 23sts. Join with a ss.

Round 3: 1ch (do not count as st), 1dc into each st to end. Join with a ss.

Round 4: Rep Round 3 a further 3 times.

MAKING UP

Press as described in Crochet Basics (see page 14).

RAFFIA CLUTCH

DESIGNED BY SAMANTA FORNINO

Here's an essential summer clutch bag that is ideal for glamorous alfresco dining. The bag is made in one piece and then sewn along the sides, so it's simple and quick to make.

SKILL LEVEL: INTERMEDIATE

YOU'LL NEED

YARN

No. 3 lightweight raffia yarn
(shown in Wool and the Gang Ra Ra Raffia)
A – 1 x 100g Desert Palm

No. 3 lightweight yarn
(shown in We Are Knitters Pima Cotton)
B – 1 x 100g Mint

HOOK

4.5mm (US 7)

HABERDASHERY

1 x 1in (25mm) metal snap button

RAFFIA CLUTCH

SIZE
Approximately 13½in (35cm) wide x 7½in (19cm) high.

TENSION
15sts and 14 rows to 4in (10cm), measured over double crochet using a 4.5mm (no. 9) hook.

METHOD
SPECIAL INSTRUCTIONS
Puff stitch (puff st) – yarn over and insert the hook into the next stitch. Yarn over and pull through 5 times (11 loops on hook). Yarn over and pull through all the loops on hook. Make 1ch.

CLUTCH
Using the 4.5mm hook and yarn A, make 50ch.
Row 1(RS): 1dc into 2nd ch from hook, 1dc into each ch to end, turn. 49sts.
Rows 2–10: 1ch (do not count as st), 1dc into every st to end. Turn.
Row 11: 1ch (do not count as st), 12dc, add yarn B, 1 puff st in B, 4dc in yarn A, 15dc in yarn B,

4dc in yarn A, 1 puff st in yarn B, 12dc in yarn A. Turn.
Row 12: 1ch (do not count as st), 11dc, change to yarn B, 1 puff st in yarn B, 1dc in yarn A, 1 puff st in yarn B, 4dc in yarn A, 13dc in yarn B, 4dc in yarn A, 1 puff st in yarn B, 1dc in yarn A, 1 puff st in B, 11dc in yarn A. Turn.
Row 13: Using yarn A, 1ch (do not count as st), 10dc in yarn A, 1 puff st in yarn B, 3dc in yarn A, 1 puff st in yarn B, 4dc in yarn A, 1dc in yarn B, 4dc in yarn A, 1 puff st in yarn B, 3dc in yarn A, 1 puff st in yarn B, 10dc in yarn A. Turn.
Row 14: Using yarn A, 1ch (do not count as st), 9dc in yarn A, 1 puff st in yarn B, 5dc in yarn A, 1 puff st in yarn B, 4dc in yarn A, 9dc in yarn B, 4dc in yarn A, 1 puff st in yarn B, 5dc in yarn A, 1 puff st in yarn B, 9dc in yarn A. Turn.
Row 15: Using yarn A, 1ch (do not count as st), 8dc in yarn A, 1 puff st in yarn B, 7dc in yarn A, 1 puff st in yarn B, 4dc in yarn A, 7dc in yarn B, 4dc in yarn A, 1 puff st in yarn B, 7dc in yarn A, 1 puff st in yarn B, 8dc in yarn A. Turn.
Row 16: Using yarn A, 1ch (do not count as st), 7dc in yarn A, 1 puff st, in yarn B, 9dc in yarn A,

1 puff st in yarn B, 4dc in yarn A, 5dc in yarn B, 4dc in yarn A, 1 puff st in yarn B, 9dc in yarn A, 1 puff st in yarn B, 7dc in yarn A. Turn.

Row 17: Using yarn A, 1ch (do not count as st), 6dc in yarn A, 1 puff st in B, 11dc in yarn A, 1 puff st in yarn B, 4dc in yarn A, 3dc in yarn B, 4dc in yarn A, 1 puff st in yarn B, 11dc in yarn A, 1 puff st in yarn B, 6dc in yarn A. Turn.

Row 18: Using yarn A, 1ch (do not count as st), 5dc in yarn A, 1 puff st in yarn B, 13dc in yarn A, 1 puff st in yarn B, 4dc in yarn A, 1dc in yarn B, 4d in yarn A, 1 puff st in yarn B, 13dc in yarn A, 1 puff st in yarn B, 5dc in yarn A. Turn.

Row 19: Using yarn A, 1ch (do not count as st), 4dc in yarn A, 1 puff st in yarn B, 15dc in yarn A, 1 puff st in yarn B, 7dc yarn A, 1 puff st in yarn B, 15dc in yarn A, 1 puff st in yarn B, 4dc in yarn A. Turn.

Row 20: Using yarn A, 1ch (do not count as st), 3dc in yarn A, 1 puff st in yarn B, 17dc in yarn A, 1 puff st in yarn B, 5dc in yarn A, 1 puff st in yarn B, 17dc in yarn A, 1 puff st in yarn B, 3dc in yarn A. Turn.

Row 21: Using yarn A, 1ch (do not count as st), 2dc in yarn A, 1 puff st in yarn B, 19dc in yarn A, 1 puff st in yarn B, 3dc in yarn A, 1 puff st in yarn B, 19dc in yarn A, 1 puff st in yarn B, 2dc in yarn A. Turn.

Row 22: Using yarn A, 1ch (do not count as st), 1dc in yarn A, 1 puff st in yarn B, 21dc in yarn A, 1 puff st in B, 1dc in A, 1 puff st in B, 21dc in A, 1 puff st in yarn B, 1dc in yarn A. Turn.

Row 23: Using yarn B, 1ch (do not count as st), 1 puff st in yarn B, 23dc in yarn A, change to yarn B, 1 puff st in yarn B, 23dc in yarn A, 1 puff st in yarn B. Turn.
Change to yarn A.

Rows 23–46: 1ch (do not count as st), 1dc into every st to end. Turn.

Row 47: Add yarn B, 1ch (do not count as st), 1 puff st in yarn B, 23dc in yarn A, 1 puff st in yarn B, 23dc in yarn A, 1 puff st in yarn B. Turn.

Row 48: Using yarn A, 1ch (do not count as st), 1dc in yarn A, 1 puff st in yarn B, 21dc in yarn A, 1 puff st in yarn B, 1dc in yarn A, 1 puff st in yarn B, 21dc in yarn A, 1 puff st in yarn B, 1dc in yarn A. Turn.

Row 49: Using yarn A, 1ch (do not count as st), 2dc in yarn A, 1 puff st in yarn B, 19dc in yarn A, 1 puff st in yarn B, 3dc in yarn A, 1 puff st in yarn B, 19dc in yarn A, 1 puff st in yarn B, 2dc in yarn A. Turn.

Row 50: Using yarn A, 1ch (do not count as st), 3dc in yarn A, 1 puff st in yarn B, change to yarn A 17dc in yarn A, 1 puff st in yarn B, 5dc in yarn A, 1 puff st in yarn B, 17dc in yarn A, 1 puff st in yarn B, 3dc in yarn A. Turn.

Row 51: Using yarn A, 1ch (do not count as st), 4dc in yarn A, 1 puff st in yarn B, 15dc in yarn A, 1 puff st in yarn B, 7dc in yarn A, 1 puff st in yarn B, 15dc in yarn A, 1 puff st in yarn B, 4dc in yarn A. Turn.

Row 52: Using yarn A, 1ch (do not count as st), 5dc in yarn A, 1 puff st in yarn B, 13dc in yarn A, 1 puff st in yarn B, 4dc in yarn A, 1dc in yarn B, 4dc in yarn A, 1 puff st in yarn B, 13dc in yarn A, 1 puff st in yarn B, 5dc in yarn A. Turn.

Row 53: Using yarn A, 1ch (do not count as st), 6dc in yarn A, 1 puff st in yarn B, 11dc in yarn A, 1 puff st in yarn B, 4dc in yarn A, 3dc in yarn B, 4dc in yarn A, 1 puff st in yarn B, 11dc in yarn A, 1 puff st in yarn B, 6dc in yarn A. Turn.

Row 54: Using yarn A, 1ch (do not count as st), 7dc in yarn A, 1 puff st in yarn B, 9dc in yarn A, 1 puff st, in yarn B, 4dc in yarn A, 5dc in yarn B, 4dc in yarn A, 1 puff st in yarn B, 9dc in yarn A, 1 puff st in yarn B, 7dc in yarn A. Turn.

Row 55: Using yarn A, 1ch (do not count as st), 8dc in yarn A, 1 puff st in yarn B, 7dc in yarn A, 1 puff st in yarn B, 4dc in yarn A, 7dc in yarn B, 4dc in yarn A, 1 puff st in yarn B, 7dc in yarn A, 1 puff st in yarn B, 8dc in yarn A. Turn.
(continued overleaf)

Row 56: Using yarn A, 1ch (do not count as st), 9dc, 1 puff st in yarn B, 5dc in yarn A, 1 puff st in yarn B, 4dc in yarn A, 9dc in yarn B, 4dc in yarn A, 1 puff st in yarn B, 5dc in yarn A, 1 puff st in yarn B, 9dc in yarn A. Turn.

Row 57: Using yarn A, 1ch (do not count as st), 10dc in yarn A, 1 puff st in yarn B, 3dc in yarn A, 1 puff st in yarn B, 4dc in yarn A, 11dc in yarn B, 4dc in yarn A, 1 puff st in yarn B, 3dc in yarn A, 1 puff st in yarn B, 10dc in yarn A. Turn.

Row 58: Using yarn A, 1ch (do not count as st), 11dc in yarn A, 1 puff st in yarn B, 1dc in yarn A. Change to yarn B. 1 puff st in yarn B, 4dc in yarn A, 13dc in B, 4dc in A, 1 puff st in B, 1dc in A, 1 puff st in yarn B, 1dc in yarn A. Turn.

Row 59: Using yarn A, 1ch (do not count as st), 12dc in yarn A, 1 puff st in yarn B, 4dc in yarn A, 15dc in yarn B, 4dc in yarn A, 1 puff st in yarn B, 12dc in yarn A. Turn.

MAKING UP

Join yarn B with a ss to any st and dc evenly around the edge (excluding Row 59). Fasten off and weave in the ends.

Sew the side panels from Row 1 to Row 46. Sew the two metal buttons in the centre of the bag, between Rows 5–9 and Rows 53–57.

COTTON SHOPPER

DESIGNED BY EMMA OSMOND

Ideal for shopping, this robust and spacious shopper features strong handles for easy and safe carrying. With its flexible structure, this carrier is deceptive and can hold a lot more than you would think.

SKILL LEVEL: INTERMEDIATE

YOU'LL NEED

YARN
No. 1 super fine cotton yarn
(shown in Anchor Creativa Fino 4ply)
3 x 50g Col. 0269

HOOK
3.5mm (E/4)

HABERDASHERY
Large-eyed darning needle

COTTON SHOPPER

SIZE

Approximately 19in (49cm) wide × 12in (30cm) high.

TENSION

20sts and 30 rows to 4in (10cm), measured over dc using a 3.5mm hook.

5.5 arches and 12.5 rows in net stitch = approximately 4in (10cm) using a 3.5mm hook.

METHOD

SPECIAL INSTRUCTIONS

Net stitch – work over any number of stitches following chart A.

SHOPPER

Using the 3.5mm hook, make 27ch.

Work in rows following chart A for your chosen size, work all repeats as specified in the chart (see page 116). After Row 87, do not cut the yarn, but turn.

LEFT-SIDE EDGING

Next row: 1ch (does not count as st), work as shown for Row 88 in chart A. Cut the yarn and fasten off.

RIGHT-SIDE EDGING

Join the yarn on the right at the base of the 1st dc of the 1st row and work as follows: 1ch (does not count as st), continue as shown for Row 89 in chart A. Cut the yarn and fasten off.

HANDLE (MAKE 2)

Using the 2.5mm hook, make 4ch, work following chart B (see page 116) for your chosen size. Repeat Rows 2 and 3 until the handle measures 18in (45cm). Cut the yarn and fasten off.

MAKING UP

Fold the bag in half and sew the side seams as shown in chart C (see page 116) for the chosen size. Begin from points A–A1 and B–B1 and sew up to the fold.

Sew the short ends of the handles to the wrong side with invisible stitches. Start from the beginning of the dc edge, and line up the sides of the handles with the side openings of the shopper.

(continued overleaf)

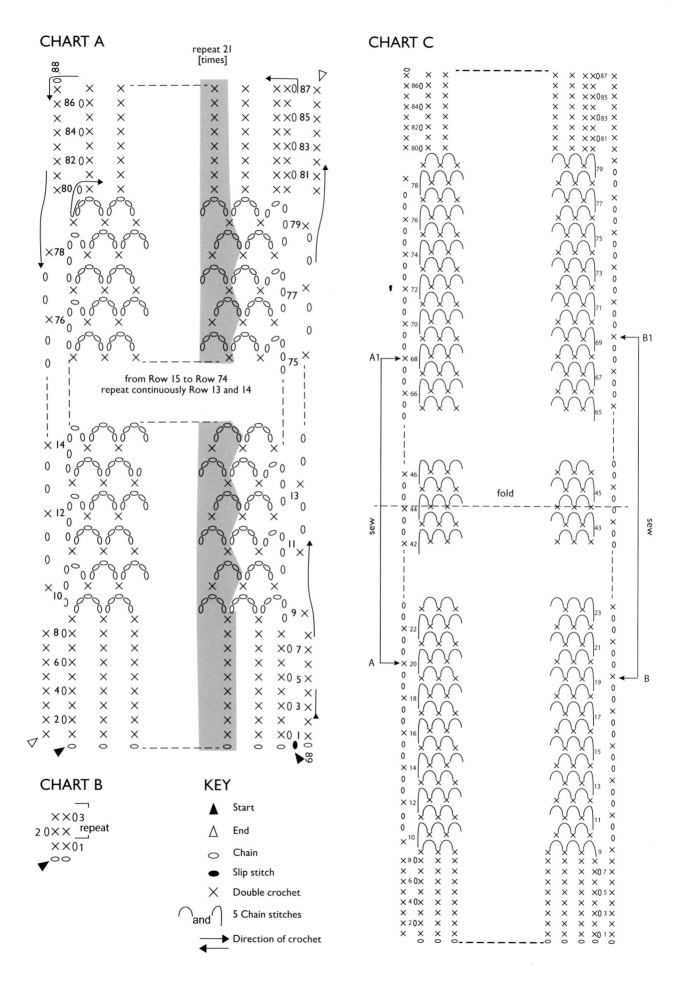

CHART A

88

repeat 21
[times]

87

86
85
84
83
82
81
80
79
78
77
76
75

from Row 15 to Row 74
repeat continuously Row 13 and 14

14
13
12
11
10
9
8 — 7
6 — 5
4 — 3
2 — 1

88

CHART B

repeat

20 — 3
20 — 1

KEY

▲ Start

△ End

⬭ Chain

⬬ Slip stitch

✕ Double crochet

⌒ and ⌒ 5 Chain stitches

→ Direction of crochet
←

CHART C

87
86
85
84
83
82
81
80
79
78
77
76
75
74
73
72
71
70
69
68   A1 →   ← B1
67
66
65

46
45
44   fold
43
42

sew   sew

23
22
21
20   A →   ← B
19
18
17
16
15
14
13
12
11
10
9
8 — 7
6 — 5
4 — 3
2 — 1

RAINBOW CLUTCH

DESIGNED BY SAN BEE

Learn new skills by making this rainbow clutch with a wrist strap. It's guaranteed to make the people around you smile. It has a retro feel that combines vibrant colours and crochet – you can't get better than that!

SKILL LEVEL: INTERMEDIATE

YOU'LL NEED

YARN
No. 3 lightweight yarn
(shown in Rowan Cotton Glacé DK)
A – 1 x 50g Blackcurrant 862
B – 1 x 50g Cobalt 850
C – 1 x 50g Mineral 856
D – 1 x 50g Persimmon 832
E – 1 x 50g Poppy 741
F – 3 x 50g Dawn Grey 831

HOOK
5mm (US H/8)

HABERDASHERY
1 x 1in (25mm) metal snap button
Large-eyed darning needle

RAINBOW CLUTCH

SIZE
Approximately 10½in (27cm) wide × 5½in (14cm) high.

TENSION
17sts and 14 rows to 4in (10cm), measured over extended double crochet using a 5mm (US H/8) hook.

METHOD
SPECIAL INSTRUCTIONS

3rd loop htr – where the pattern indicates, working into the 3rd loop. This is the loop that sits horizontally underneath the regular loop at the top of the stitch.

Adjustable loop – wrap yarn around your index finger, over the top of the finger anticlockwise and all the way around the finger. Slide the loop off your finger and work the sts for the first round into this loop. Pull tightly closed and ss into 1st st. edc (extended double crochet) insert the hook from front to back into the next st, yarn over and draw the loop through, yarn over and draw through the first loop only, forming a chain stitch, yarn over and draw through both loops on the hook.

RAINBOW FLAP

Using a 5mm hook and yarn A with 2 strands held together, make an adjustable loop (see Special Instructions, left).

Row 1: 1ch (does not count as st), 5dc into loop, turn.

Row 2: 1ch (does not count as st), 1dc into next st, 2dc into next 3sts, 1dc into last st, turn. 8sts.

Row 3: 1ch (does not count as st), 1dc into next st, (2dc into next st, 1dc into next 2sts) twice, 2dc into last st, turn. 11sts.

Row 4: 1ch (do not count as st), 1htr into next 3st, 2htr into next st, 1htr into next 2st, 2htr into next st, 1htr into next 3sts, 2htr into last st, turn. 14sts.

Change to yarn B. The next row is worked into the 3rd loop of the htrs in the previous row. Join with ss to the first st of Row 4.

Row 5: 1ch (does not count as st), 1dc into the next 2sts, (2dc into next st, 1dc into next 3sts) 3 times, turn. 17sts.

Row 6: 1ch (does not count as st), (2dc into next st, 1dc in next 5sts) twice, 2dc into next st, 1dc into next 4sts, turn. 20sts.

Row 7: 1ch (does not count as st), (2dc into next st, 1dc in next 6sts) twice, 2dc into next st, 1dc into next 5sts, turn. 23sts.

Row 8: 1ch (does not count as st), (2htr into next st, 1htr into next 7sts) twice, 2htr into next st, 1htr into next 6sts, turn. 26sts.

Change to yarn C. The next row is worked into the 3rd loop of the htrs in previous row. Join with ss into 1st st of Row 8.

Row 9: 1ch (does not count as st), (2dc into next st, 1dc in next 8sts) twice, 2dc into next st, 1dc into next 7sts, turn. 29sts.

Row 10: 1ch (does not count as st), (2dc into next st, 1dc in next 9sts) twice, 2dc into next st, 1dc into next 8sts, turn. 32sts.

Row 11: 1ch (does not count as st), 2dc into next st, 1dc into next 11sts, 2dc into next st, 1dc into next 9sts, 2dc into next st, 1dc into next 10sts, turn. 35sts.

Row 12: 1ch (does not count as st), 2htr into next st, 1htr into next 10sts, 2htr into next st, 1htr into next 11sts, 2htr into next st, 1htr into next 11sts, turn. 38sts.

Change to yarn D. The next row is worked into the 3rd loop of the htrs in previous row. Join with ss to first st of Row 12.

Row 13: 1ch (does not count as st), 2dc into next st, 1dc into next 12sts, 2dc into next, 1dc into next 11sts, 2dc into next st, 1dc into next 12sts, turn. 41sts.

Row 14: 1ch (does not count as st), 2dc into next st, 1dc into next 13sts, 2dc into next st, 1dc into next 11sts, 2dc into next st, 1dc into next 14sts, turn. 44sts.

Row 15: 1ch (does not count as st), 2dc into next st, 1dc into next 14sts, 2dc into next st, 1dc in next 11sts, 2dc into next st, 1dc into next 16sts, turn. 47sts.

Row 16: 1ch (does not count as st), 2htr into next st, 1htr into next 16sts, 2htr into next st, 1htr into next 10sts, 2htr into next st, 1htr into next 18sts, turn. 50sts.

Change to yarn E. The next row is worked into the 3rd loop of the htrs in previous row. Join with ss to first st of Row 16.

Row 17: 1ch (does not count as st), 2dc into next st, 1dc into next 17sts, 2dc into next st, 1dc into next 10sts, 2dc into next st, 1dc into next 20sts, turn. 53sts.

Row 18: 1ch (does not count as st), 2dc into next st, 1dc in next 18sts, 2dc in next st, 1dc in next 11sts, 2dc in next st, 1dc into next 21sts, turn. 55sts.

Row 19: 1ch (does not count as st), 2dc into next st, 1dc into next 19sts, 2dc into next st, 1dc in next 12sts, 2dc into next st, 1dc into next 22sts, turn. 58sts.

Row 20: 1ch (does not count as st), 2htr into next st, 1htr into next 20sts, 2htr into next st, 1htr into next 13sts, 2htr into next st, 1htr into next 23sts, turn. 61sts.

Row 21: 1ss in every st. Fasten off.

(continued overleaf)

CLUTCH

Using a 5mm hook and 2 strands of yarn F held together, make 43ch.

Row 1: Working in the back bumps of the starting ch, edc in each ch, turn.

Rows 2–38: 1ch, edc in each st, turn. Fasten off.

WRIST BAND

Using a 5mm hook and 4 strands of yarn F held together, make 45ch. Fasten off.

MAKING UP

Lightly block (see page 14) all pieces.

With the RS facing the rainbow flap, attach the panel to the shorter edge of the main clutch body using 42ss.

Using a 5mm hook and one strand of yarn F, make 43ch and sew to the top of the clutch.

With the RS facing inwards, fold the clutch in half and sew the side seams.

Attach the metal snaps to the clutch and flap.

Sew the wrist band into one corner of the clutch.

> *Tip*
> This pattern uses two strands of yarn held together to ensure the resulting fabric is firm and dense. You could make a matching coin purse by working the pattern in a single strand of yarn and using a smaller hook.

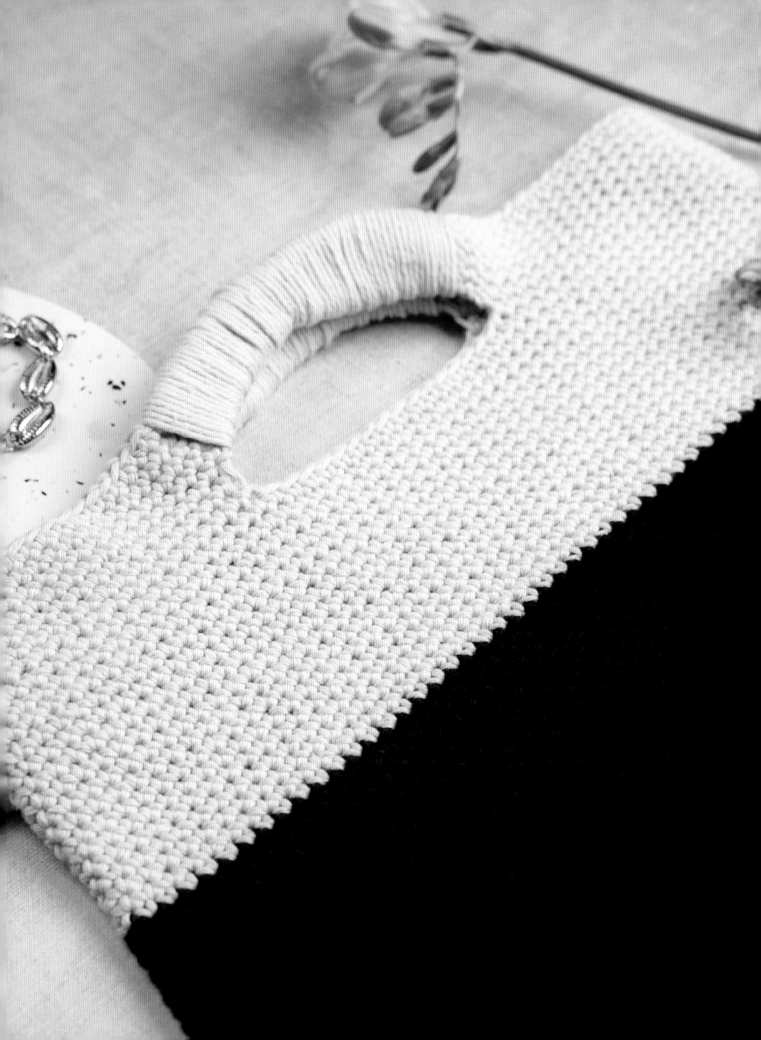

SIMPLE SHOPPER
DESIGNED BY EMMA WRIGHT

A beginner project with handles that are reinforced to help withstand everyday wear and tear. Its elegant two-tone design means it can also be used for more formal occasions, such as a business lunch or office meeting.

SKILL LEVEL: EASY

YOU'LL NEED

YARN
No. 4 medium-weight yarn
(shown in Paintbox Yarns Cotton Aran)
A – 2 x 50g Pure Black 602
B – 2 x 50g Vanilla Cream 608

HOOK
5mm (US H/8)

HABERDASHERY
Large-eyed sewing needle
1 x stitch marker

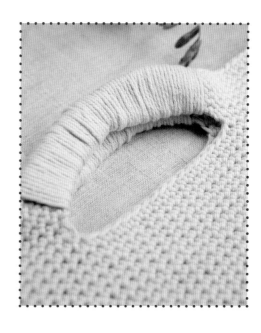

SIMPLE SHOPPER

SIZE
14in (35cm) wide × 10in (26 cm) high.

TENSION
15sts and 20 rows to 4in (10cm), measured over double crochet using a 5mm hook.

METHOD
BAG
Using a 5mm hook and yarn A, make 51ch.
Round 1: 4dc into 2nd ch from hook, 1dc into next 48sts, 4dc into last ch, turn work upside down and work into the other side of beg ch, miss 1st ch, 1dc in next 48sts, work ss into first dc made to join round. 104sts.
Round 2: Place a stitch marker to indicate the beg/end of the round. 1dc in every st (you will now work in a spiral). Move the stitch marker up with every round.
Rounds 3–24: Repeat Round 2, working a ss to join the round after last st of Round 24 only.

Change to yarn B.
Rounds 1–16: Work 16 rounds of dc in a spiral.
Round 17: Work 9dc, move the stitch marker to this point.
Round 18: 1dc into next 18sts, 20ch, miss next 16sts, 1dc into next 36sts, ch20, miss next 16sts, 20ch, 1dc into next 18sts.
Round 19: 1dc into next 18sts, work 20dc into 20ch-sp, 1dc into next 36sts, work 20dc into 20ch-sp, 1dc into next 18sts. 112sts.
Rounds 20–25: Work 5 rounds of dc, joining the last round with a ss.
Fasten off.

MAKING UP
Fasten off all loose ends.

Wrap a long strand of yarn B neatly from the beginning to the end of each handle.

SMALL CLUTCH BAG
DESIGNED BY SAMANTA FORNINO

A small clutch that is useful for storing personal items or as a holder for make-up when you're out and about. The bag is made in two parts and then sewn together. It may be small, but with its unusual geometrical pattern, this bag will be the centre of attention.

SKILL LEVEL: INTERMEDIATE

YOU'LL NEED

YARN
No. 3 lightweight yarn
(shown in Rowan Creative Linen)
A – 1 x 100g Mustard 647
B – 1 x 100g Cloud 620

HOOK
5mm (US H/8)

HABERDASHERY
1 x ¾in (20mm) metal snap button or 8½in
   (22cm) long zip
Large-eyed darning needle

SMALL CLUTCH BAG

SIZE

Approximately 8½in (22cm) wide × 9in (23cm) long.

TENSION

15sts and 10 rows to 4in (10cm), measured over half treble crochet using a 5mm (US H/8) hook and 2 strands of yarn held together.

METHOD

SPECIAL INSTRUCTIONS

Back loop only (BLO) – insert hook into back loop only of next st and make stitch indicated.

Pattern note – when a new colour is introduced, lay the other colour over the hook, towards the back of the work, and trap it inside each st worked to trail non-used yarn across the row. Then, when needed, pick up the new colour and lay the old colour behind, as you did previously.

FRONT

Using the 5mm hook and 2 strands of yarn A held together, make 32ch.

Row 1 (RS): 1htr into 3rd chain from hook, 1htr into each ch to end, turn. 31sts.

Row 2: 2ch (counts as htr), 2htr, add yarn B, 25htr, pick up yarn A, 3htr. Turn.

Row 3: Work row in BLO, 2ch in yarn A (counts as htr), 2htr in yarn A, 2htr in yarn B, 9htr in yarn A, 3htr in yarn B, 9htr in yarn A, 2htr in yarn B, 3htr in yarn A. Turn.

Row 4: 2ch in yarn A (counts as htr), 3htr in yarn A, 2htr in yarn B, 7htr in yarn A, 2htr in yarn B, 1htr in yarn A, 2htr in yarn B, 7htr in yarn A, 2htr in yarn B, 4htr in yarn A. Turn.

Row 5: Work row in BLO 2ch in yarn A (counts as htr), 4htr in yarn A, 2htr in yarn B, 5htr in yarn A, 2htr in yarn B, 3htr in yarn A, 2htr in yarn B, 5htr in yarn A, 2htr in yarn B, 5htr in yarn A. Turn.

Row 6: 2ch in yarn A (counts as htr), 2htr in yarn A, 1htr in yarn B, 2htr in yarn A, 2htr in yarn B, 3htr in yarn A, 2htr in yarn B, 2htr in yarn A, 1htr in yarn B, 2htr in yarn A, 2htr in yarn B, 3htr in yarn A, 2htr in yarn B, 2htr in yarn A, 1htr in yarn B, 3htr in yarn A. Turn.

Row 7: Work row in BLO, 2ch in yarn A (counts as htr), 2htr in yarn A, 2htr in yarn B, 2htr in yarn A, 2htr in yarn B, 1htr in yarn A, 2htr in yarn B, 2htr in yarn A, 3htr in yarn B, 2htr in yarn A, 2htr in yarn B, 1htr in yarn A. 2htr in yarn B. 2htr in yarn A, 2htr in yarn B, 3htr in yarn A. Turn.

Row 8: 2ch in yarn A (counts as htr), 3htr in yarn A, 2htr in yarn B, 2htr in yarn A, 3htr in yarn B, 2htr in yarn A, 2htr in yarn B, 1htr in yarn A, 2htr in yarn B, 2htr in yarn A, 3htr in yarn B, 2htr in yarn A, 2htr in yarn B, 4htr in yarn A. Turn.

Row 9: Work row in BLO, 2ch in yarn A (counts as st), 4htr in yarn A, 2htr in yarn B, 2htr in yarn A, 1htr in yarn B, 2htr in yarn A, 2htr in yarn B, 3htr in yarn A, 2htr in yarn B, 2htr in yarn A, 1htr yarn B, 2htr in yarn A. 2htr in yarn B, 5htr in yarn A. Turn.

Row 10: 2ch in yarn A (counts as htr), 5htr in yarn A, 2htr in yarn B, 3htr in yarn A, 2htr in yarn B, 5htr in yarn A, 2htr in yarn B, 3htr in yarn A, 2htr in yarn B, 6htr in yarn A. Turn.

Row 11: Work row in BLO, 2ch in yarn A (counts as htr), 6htr in yarn A, 2htr in yarn B, 1htr in yarn A, 2htr in yarn B, 7htr in yarn A, 2htr in yarn B, 1htr in yarn A, 2htr in yarn B, 7htr in yarn A. Turn.

Row 12: 2ch in yarn A (counts as htr), 5htr in yarn A, 2htr in yarn B, 3htr in yarn A, 2htr in yarn B, 5htr in yarn A, 2htr in yarn B, 3htr in yarn A, 2htr in yarn B, 6htr in yarn A. Turn.

Row 13: Work row in BLO, 2ch in yarn A (counts as htr), 4htr in yarn A, 2htr in yarn B, 2htr in yarn A, 1htr in yarn B, 2htr in yarn A, 2htr in yarn B, 3htr in yarn A, 2htr yarn B, 2htr in yarn A, 1htr in yarn B, 2htr in yarn A. 2htr in yarn B, 5htr in yarn A. Turn.

Row 14: 2ch in yarn A (counts as htr), 3htr in yarn A, 2htr in yarn B, 2htr in yarn A, 3htr in yarn B, 2htr in yarn A, 2htr in yarn B, 1htr in yarn A, 2htr in yarn B, 2htr in yarn A, 3htr in yarn B, 2htr in yarn A. 2htr in yarn B, 4htr in yarn A. Turn.

Row 15: Work row in BLO 2ch (counts as htr), 2htr in yarn A, 2htr in yarn B, 2htr in yarn A, 2htr in yarn B, 1htr in yarn A, 2htr in yarn B, 2htr in yarn A, 3htr in yarn B, 2htr in yarn A, 2htr in yarn B, 1htr in yarn A, 2htr in yarn B, 2htr in yarn A, 2htr in yarn B, 3htr in yarn A. Turn.

Row 16: 2ch in yarn A (counts as htr), 2htr in yarn A, 1htr in yarn B, 2htr in yarn A, 2htr in yarn B, 3htr in yarn A, 2htr in yarn B, 2htr in yarn A, 1htr in yarn B, 2htr in yarn A, 2htr in yarn B, 3htr in yarn A, 2htr in yarn B, 2htr in yarn A, 1htr in yarn B, 3htr in yarn A. Turn.

Row 17: Work row in BLO 2ch in yarn A (counts as htr), 4htr in yarn A, 2htr in yarn B, 5htr in yarn A, 2htr in yarn B, 3htr in yarn A, 2htr in yarn B, 5htr in yarn A, 2htr in yarn B, 5htr in yarn A. Turn.

Row 18: 2ch in yarn A (counts as htr), 3htr in yarn A, 2htr in yarn B, 7htr in yarn A, 2htr in yarn B, 1htr in yarn A, 2htr in yarn B, 7htr in yarn A, 2htr in yarn B, 4htr in yarn A. Turn.

Row 19: Work row in BLO, 2ch in yarn A (counts as htr), 2htr in yarn A, 2htr in yarn B, 9htr in yarn A, 3htr in yarn B, 9htr in yarn A, 2htr in yarn B, 3htr in yarn A. Turn.

Row 20: 2ch in yarn A (counts as htr), 2htr in yarn A, 25htr in yarn B, 3htr in yarn A. Turn.

Row 21: Using yarn A, 1htr into each st to the end. Fasten off.
Rejoin yarn B with a ss to any st and dc evenly around edge. Fasten off and weave in the ends.

BACK
Using a 5mm hook and yarn B, make 32ch.
Row 1 (RS): 1htr into 3rd chain from hook, 1htr into each ch to end, turn. 31sts.
Rows 2–21: 1htr into each st to the end.

MAKING UP
Place the front over the back and join around 3 edges, leaving one end open for the top. Sew the snap button or the zip to the inside of the opening.

SUMMER SHOPPER
DESIGNED BY SAMANTA FORNINO

Made from chunky cotton, this versatile bag is a must-have as your go-to summer shopper. It is worked in one piece and straightforward to make. With its unusual design, it's both stylish and practical and will become a firm favourite.

SKILL LEVEL: EASY

YOU'LL NEED

YARN
No. 6 super bulky cotton yarn
(shown in Hooked Spesso Chunky Cotton)
A – 2 x 500g Noir
B – 1 x 500g Almond

No. 3 lightweight yarn for the pompoms
Approximately 10g in green, pink and light blue

HOOK
9mm (US M/13)

HABERDASHERY
45mm (1½in) pompom maker
Large-eyed darning needle

SUMMER SHOPPER

SIZE:

Approximately 18in (46cm) high x 16½in (42cm) deep.

TENSION

9sts and 5 rows to 4in (10cm), measured over double crochet using a 9mm hook.

METHOD

SPECIAL INSTRUCTIONS

Back loop only (BLO) – insert the hook into the back loop only of the next st and make the stitch indicated.

Pattern note – when a new colour is introduced, lay the other colour over the hook, towards the back of the work, and trap inside each st worked to trail non-used yarn across the row. Then, when needed, pick up the new colour and lay the old colour behind, as you did previously.

BASE

Using the 9mm hook and yarn A, make 31ch.

Row 1 (RS): 1dc into 2nd chain from hook, 1dc into each ch to end, turn. 30sts.

Rows 2–9: 1ch (does not count as st), 1dc into st to end, turn.

SIDES

Using yarn A, work in rounds around the entire edge of the rectangle as follows:

Round 10: 1ch (do not count as st), 1dc into every st and every row end around, join with ss into the first dc. 80sts.

Round 11: Work round in BLO, 2ch (counts as st), 1htr into every st to end, join with ss. 80sts. Add yarn B.

Round 12: Work round in BLO, 2ch in yarn B (counts as st), 1htr in yarn B, 2htr in yarn A, 2htr in yarn B, 2htr in yarn A, 2htr in yarn B, 2htr in yarn A, 6htr in yarn B, (2htr in A, 2htr in B) 8 times, 2htr in yarn A, 6htr in yarn B, (2htr in A, 2htr in B) 5 times, 2htr in yarn A, join with ss.

Round 13: Work round in BLO, 2ch in yarn B

(counts as st), (2htr in A, 2htr in B) 2 times, 2htr in yarn A, 8htr in yarn B, (2htr in A, 2htr in B) 3 times, 2htr in yarn A, 4htr in yarn B, (2htr in A, 2htr in B) 3 times, 2htr in yarn A, 8htr in yarn B, (2htr in A, 2htr in B) 3 times, 2htr in yarn A, 4htr in yarn B, 2htr in yarn A, 1htr in yarn B, join with ss.

Round 14: Work round in BLO, 2ch in yarn A (counts as st), 1htr in yarn A, (2htr in B, 2htr in A) 2 times, 10htr in B, (2htr in A, 2htr in B) 3 times, 1htr in yarn A, 4htr in yarn B, 1htr in yarn A, (2htr in B, 2htr in A) 3 times, 10htr in yarn B, (2htr in A, 2htr in B) 3 times, 1htr in yarn A, 4htr in yarn B, 1htr in yarn A, 2htr in yarn B, join with ss.

Round 15: Work round in BLO, 2ch in yarn A (counts as st), (2htr in B, 2htr in A) 2 times, 12htr in yarn B, (2htr in A, 2htr in B) 2 times, 2htr in yarn A, 1htr in yarn B, 1 htr in yarn A, 4htr in yarn B, 1htr in yarn A, 1htr in yarn B, 2htr in yarn A (2htr in B, 2htr in A) 2 times, 12htr in yarn B, (2htr in A, 2htr in B) 2 times, 2htr in yarn A, 1htr in yarn B, 1htr in yarn A, 4htr in yarn B, 1htr in yarn A, 1htr in yarn B, 1htr in yarn A, join with ss.

Round 16: Work round in BLO, 2ch in yarn B (counts as st), 1htr in yarn B, 2htr in yarn A, 2htr in yarn B, 2htr in yarn A, 14htr in yarn B, (2htr in A, 2htr in B) 2 times, 3htr in yarn A, 4htr in yarn B, 3htr in yarn A, (2htr in B, 2htr in A) 2 times, 14htr in yarn B, (2htr in A, 2htr in B) 2 times, 3htr in yarn A, 4htr in yarn B, 3htr in yarn A, join with ss.

Round 17: Work round in BLO, 2ch in yarn B (counts as st), 2htr in yarn A, 2htr in yarn B, 2htr in yarn A, 16htr in yarn B, (2htr in A, 2htr in B) 2 times, 2htr in yarn A, 4htr in yarn B, 2htr in yarn A, (2htr in B, 2htr in A) 2 times, 2htr in yarn A, 16 htr in yarn B,(2htr in A, 2htr in B) 2 times, 2htr in yarn A, 4htr in yarn B, 2htr in yarn A, 1htr in yarn B, join with ss.

Round 18: Work round in BLO, 2ch in yarn A (counts as st) 1htr in yarn A, 2htr in yarn B, 2htr in yarn A, 18 htr in yarn B, (2htr in A, 2htr in B) 2 times, 1htr in yarn A, 4htr in yarn B, 1htr in yarn A, (2htr in B, 2htr in A) 2 times, 18htr in

yarn B, (2htr in A, 2htr in B) 2 times, 1htr in yarn A, 4htr in yarn B, 1htr yarn A, 2htr in yarn B, join with ss.

Round 19: Work round in BLO, 2ch in yarn A (counts as st), 2htr in yarn B, 2htr in yarn A, 20htr in yarn B, 2htr in yarn A, 2htr in yarn B, 2htr in yarn A, 1htr in yarn B, 1htr in yarn A, 4htr in yarn B, 1htr in yarn A, 1htr in yarn B, 2htr in yarn A, 2htr in yarn B, 2htr in yarn A, 20htr in yarn B, 2htr in yarn A, 2htr in yarn B, 2htr in yarn A, 1htr in yarn B, 1htr in yarn A, 4htr in yarn B, 1htr in yarn A, 1htr in yarn B, 1htr in yarn A, join with ss.

Round 20: Work round in BLO, 2ch in yarn B (counts as st), 1htr in yarn B, 2htr in yarn A, 22htr in yarn B, 2htr in yarn A, 2htr in yarn B, 3htr in yarn A, 4htr in yarn B, 3htr in yarn A, 2htr in yarn B, 2htr in yarn A, 22htr in yarn B, 2htr in yarn A, 2htr in yarn B, 3htr in yarn A, 4htr in yarn B, 3htr in yarn A, join with ss.

Round 21: Work round in BLO, 2ch in yarn B (counts as st), 1htr in yarn B, 2htr in yarn A, 22htr in yarn B, (2htr in A, 2htr in B) 4 times, 2htr in yarn A, 22htr in yarn B, (2htr in A, 2htr in B) 3 times, 2htr in yarn A, join with ss.

Rounds 22–24: Work rounds in BLO (2htr in B, 2htr in A) 40 times, join with ss.
Change to yarn A only.

Round 25: 1ch (does not count as st), 1dc into every st, join with ss.

Round 26: 1ch (does not count as st), 10dc, miss 10sts, 30ch, 30dc, miss 10sts, 30ch, 20dc, join with ss.

Round 27: 1ch (does not count as st), 1dc into every st to end, join with ss. 120sts.

MAKING UP
Make three small pompoms using the pompom maker and different coloured yarns. Leave a long cord when the pompoms are complete and thread this through a large-eyed sewing needle. Sew this cord into one of the handles at the side of the bag, leaving 2–2½in (5–6cm) between the pompoms and the seam.

STRIPED BAG

DESIGNED BY EMMA OSMOND

With its rope-style handles and open pattern effect, this carry bag is a summer essential. Ideal for trips to the beach or for exploring new places, choose bright, tropical colours to complement your favourite hot-weather outfits.

SKILL LEVEL: INTERMEDIATE

YOU'LL NEED

YARN

No. 1 super fine yarn
(shown in Anchor Creativa Fino 4ply)
A – 4 x 50g 0251
B – 2 x 50g 00105
C – 2 x 50g 0434
D – 1 x 50g 0246
E – 1 x 50g 0434

HOOK

3mm

HABERDASHERY

4 x stitch markers
Large-eyed darning needle

STRIPED BAG

SIZE:
19in (48cm) high x 12in (30cm) wide.

TENSION
22sts and 26 rows to 4in (10cm), measured over double crochet using a 3mm hook.

METHOD
SPECIAL INSTRUCTIONS
Popcorn – work 4tr into next st, drop the loop from the hook, insert the hook from the front into the top of the first of these tr, pick up the dropped loop and draw through tr, 1ch to secure popcorn.

Make bobble (MB) – *yarn over, insert the hook into the stitch and pull through the loop, yarn over pull through 2 loops; rep from * until 6 loops are on your hook, yarn over and pull through all 6 loops.

FAN AND POPCORN STRIPE
Row 1: 1ch (does not count as st), 1dc into next st, *1ch, miss 3sts, into the next st (1tr, 1ch) 3 times, miss 3sts, 1dc into next st; rep from * to the end, turn.
Row 2: 6ch (counts as 1tr, 3ch), miss 1tr, 1dc into next tr, *3ch, 1 popcorn into next dc, 3ch, miss 1tr, 1dc into next tr, rep from * to last dc, 3ch 1tr into last dc, turn.

BOBBLE STRIPE
Row 1: 1ch (does not count as st), 1dc into next tr, *3dc into next ch-sp, 1dc into next dc, 3dc into next ch-sp, 1dc into next popcorn; rep from * to last popcorn, 3dc into next ch-sp, 1dc into next dc, 4dc into next ch-sp, turn.
Row 2: 1ch (does not count as st), 1dc into each st to end, turn.
Row 3: 1ch (does not count as st), 1dc into next 2sts, * MB, 1dc into next 3sts, rep from * to last 3sts, MB, 1dc into next 2sts, turn.
Row 4: 1ch (does not count as st), 1dc into each st to the end, turn.
Row 5: Rep last row once more.

BASE

Using the 3mm hook and yarn A, make 89ch.

Row 1 (RS): 1dc into 2nd ch from hook, 1dc into each ch to end, turn. 88sts.

Row 2: 1ch (does not count as st), 1dc into each st to end, turn.

Rep last row 30 times more.

Fasten off.

SIDE PANEL (MAKE 2)

Using the 3mm hook and yarn A, make 106ch.

Row 1 (RS): 1dc into 2nd ch from hook, 1dc into each ch to end, turn. 105sts.

Row 2: 1ch (does not count as st), 1dc into each st to end, turn.

Rep last row until work measures 3cm (1¼in), ending with a WS row.

Change to yarn B.

Work Fan and Popcorn Stripe.

Change to yarn D.

Work Bobble Stripe.

Change to yarn B.

Work Fan and Popcorn Stripe.

Change to yarn A.

Row 1: 1ch (does not count as st), 1dc into next tr, *3dc into next ch-sp, 1dc into next dc, 3dc into next ch-sp, 1dc into next popcorn; rep from * to last popcorn, 3dc into next ch-sp, 1dc into next dc, 4dc into next ch-sp, turn. 105sts.

Row 2: 1ch (does not count as st), 1dc into each st to the end, turn.

Rep last row until work measures 3cm (1¼in), ending with a WS row.

Change to yarn C.

Work Fan and Popcorn Stripe.

Change to yarn E.

Work Bobble Stripe.

Change to yarn C.

Work Fan and Popcorn Stripe.

Change to yarn A.

Row 1: 1ch (does not count as st), 1dc into next tr, *3dc into next ch-sp, 1dc into next dc, 3dc into

next ch-sp, 1dc into next popcorn; rep from * to last popcorn, 3dc into next ch-sp, 1dc into next dc, 4dc into next ch-sp, turn. 105sts.

Row 2: 1ch (does not count as st), 1dc into each st to the end, turn.

Rep last row until work measures 3cm (1¼in), ending with a WS row.

Change to yarn B.

Work Fan and Popcorn Stripe.

Change to yarn D.

Work Bobble Stripe.

Change to yarn B.

Work Fan and Popcorn Stripe.

Change to yarn A.

Row 1: 1ch (does not count as st), 1dc into next tr, *3dc into next ch-sp, 1dc into next dc, 3dc into next ch-sp, 1dc into next popcorn; rep from * to last popcorn, 3dc into next ch-sp, 1dc into next dc, 4dc into next ch-sp, turn. 105sts.

Row 2: 1ch (does not count as st), 1dc into each st to the end, turn.

Change to yarn B.

Row 3: 1ch (does not count as st), 1dc into each st to end, turn.

Rep last row once more.

Change to yarn D.

Row 1: 1ch (does not count as st), 1dc into each st to the end, turn.

Rep last row once more.

Change to yarn B.

Row 1: 1ch (does not count as st), 1dc into each st to the end, turn.

Rep last row once more.

Change to yarn C.

Row 1: 1ch (does not count as st), 1dc into each st to the end, turn.

Rep last row once more.

Change to yarn B.

Row 1: 1ch (does not count as st), 1dc into each st to the end, turn.

Rep last row once more.

Change to yarn A.

Row 1: 1ch (does not count as st), 1dc into each st to the end, turn.
Rep last row once more.
Fasten off.

MAKING UP
Press as described in Crochet Basics (see page 14).

With the RS facing out, pin each end of the side panel to the middle of the shorter edge of the base. Sew the side panels around the edge of the base using a mattress stitch.

Sew the side seams matching the pattern.

HANDLE (MAKE 2)
For each handle, using yarn B, cut eight lengths of each yarn 70¾in (180cm) long and tie a knot at each end. Secure one end and twist the other end until the cord starts to twist around itself, until it measures approximately 47¼in (120cm). Take the centre of the cord with your free hand so that it twists from the middle, and continue to twist the cord until the entire length has a firm twist.

Using the photograph on page 141 as your reference, thread the end of each cord through the crochet fabric and tie a knot in the ends of the cord to prevent it sliding back through the crochet fabric.

RESOURCES

Yarns

Anchor – anchorcrafts.com
Hoooked – hoookedyarn.com
Knit Purl Crochet – kpcyarn.com
Ophelia Italy – opheliaitaly.com
Paintbox Yarns – paintboxyarns.com
Rowan Yarns – knitrowan.com
Wool and the Gang – woolandthegang.com

Haberdashery and basic equipment

Amazon – amazon.com
Hobbycraft – hobbycraft.co.uk
John Lewis – johnlewis.com

ACKNOWLEDGEMENTS

I would like to thank everybody who helped me put this book together. Most importantly, I'd like to thank my wonderful husband, who put up with all of the late nights I spent writing it and supported me throughout the process. Special thanks also go to the amazing designers who contributed their skills and designs to this project. It was a pleasure to work with such creative minds to make this varied book of designs a reality. Finally, I would like to thank the team at GMC and Quail for bringing my ideas to life and making this book possible.

Emma Osmond
@quail_studio

To find out more about the designers featured in this book, visit their Instagram profiles listed below:

Louise Ballanos
@handylittleme

San Bee
@loopsanpic

Samanta Fornino
@followthecrochet

Kathy Merrick
@kathrynhmerrick

Amy Parker
@hookedbyhandmade

Emma Wright
@emmaknitted

INDEX

To order a book, contact:

GMC Publications Ltd
Castle Place, 166 High Street,
Lewes, East Sussex,
BN7 1XU
United Kingdom
Tel: +44 (0)1273 488005
www.gmcbooks.com